Mark Twain

THE PROFILES IN LITERATURE SERIES

GENERAL EDITOR: B. C. SOUTHAM, M.A., B.LITT. (OXON.)
*Formerly Department of English, Westfield College,
University of London*

Volumes in this series include

Mark Twain

by I. M. Walker
Lecturer in American Literature
University of Manchester

LONDON
ROUTLEDGE & KEGAN PAUL

First published 1970
by Routledge & Kegan Paul Limited
Broadway House, 68-74 Carter Lane
London, E.C.4
Printed in Great Britain
by Northumberland Press Ltd
Gateshead
© I. M. Walker 1970
ISBN 0 7100 6812 3 (c)
ISBN 0 7100 6813 1 (p)

The Profiles in Literature Series

This series is designed to provide the student of literature and the general reader with a brief and helpful introduction to the major novelists and prose writers in English, American and foreign literature.

Each volume will provide an account of an individual author's writing career and works, through a series of carefully chosen extracts illustrating the major aspects of the author's art. These extracts are accompanied by commentary and analysis, drawing attention to particular features of the style and treatment. There is no pretence, of course, that a study of extracts can give a sense of the works as a whole, but this selective approach enables the reader to focus his attention upon specific features, and to be informed in his approach by experienced critics and scholars who are contributing to the series.

The volumes will provide a particularly helpful and practical form of introduction to writers whose works are extensive or which present special problems for the modern reader, who can then proceed with a sense of his bearings and an informed eye for the writer's art.

An important feature of these books is the extensive reference list of the author's works and the descriptive list of the most useful biographies, commentaries and critical studies.

B.C.S.

Contents

CONTENTS

Mark Twain: His life and works

Ernest Hemingway's remark in *Green Hills of Africa* that
'All modern American literature comes from one book
by Mark Twain called *Huckleberry Finn*.... There was
nothing before. There has been nothing as good since' is,
of course, an exaggeration, but it probably reflects the
experience of many readers whose acquaintance with
American literature begins with Mark Twain's classic
novels of childhood, *The Adventures of Tom Sawyer* and
Huckleberry Finn. But Twain did not see himself primarily
as a children's writer; of *Tom Sawyer* he said: 'It is *not*
a boy's book at all. It will only be read by adults. It is
only written for adults.' Whatever Twain may have
intended, his books have delighted generations of children;
yet by regarding him solely as a 'children's classic' the
older reader is in danger of missing much of the com-
plexity and seriousness of his work. To begin with, it is
important to realize that 'Mark Twain' is both a literary
character in his own right and an extension of his creator,
Samuel Langhorne Clemens (1835-1910). Clemens was
basically an autobiographical writer, and 'Mark Twain'
was the comic persona through which he gave imaginative
expression to his own experience.

'I was born', Mark Twain wrote, 'in the almost invisible

village of Florida, Monroe County, Missouri. My parents removed to Missouri in the early "thirties"; I do not remember just when for I was not born then and cared nothing for such things.' Shortly afterwards his family moved again, this time to the small Mississippi river town of Hannibal, Missouri, where Clemens spent his boyhood. Memories of Hannibal as it was during the 1840s were a vital source of inspiration for Clemens, though his feelings towards the town and its people were ambivalent, even contradictory. In 'Old Times on the Mississippi' it is associated with innocence and joy, a 'white town drowsing in the sunshine'; in *The Adventures of Tom Sawyer* it is St. Petersburg, an idyllic village where childhood fantasies come true; but in *The Adventures of Huckleberry Finn* the imaginative re-creation of Hannibal is shabby and mean, and elements of violence, cruelty and hypocrisy lie beneath the placid surface of the village. In the later fiction Hannibal is disguised as Hadleyburg, the town whose boasted innocence and virtue are exposed as a sham, or Dawson's Landing, the morally bankrupt setting of *Pudd'n-head Wilson*. It was in Hannibal too, that Clemens first encountered slavery (his family owned slaves), and slavery was to become an important theme in his fiction.

In 1848 Clemens's elementary schooling came to an end due to family poverty (his father had died in 1847), and he went to work as a printer's apprentice. For the next nine years he worked as an itinerant printer and occasional journalist, until he met Horace Bixby who worked as a pilot on the Mississippi. Clemens was fired with an ambition to emulate his boyhood heroes, and he began the arduous task of 'learning' the river under Bixby's supervision. The outbreak of the Civil War brought an end to his career as a pilot, but already he had accumulated the experience that went into his greatest

2

writing: the material of the river and the town on its banks.

The Civil War took up little of Clemens's attention; in 1861 he left with his erratic elder brother, Orion, for the new territory of Nevada. The flush times of the silver bonanza excited and fascinated him, and he quickly established a local reputation as a comic journalist. The name 'Mark Twain' first appeared in a comic sketch written for the *Territorial Enterprise* of Virginia City, Nevada, in February 1863. It marks Clemens's discovery of his comic identity. In choosing to write under a pseudonym Clemens was responding to established conventions of popular American humour; he knew and admired such masters of the arts of comic oration and journalism as Petroleum V. Nasby (David Ross Locke), Josh Billings (Henry W. Shaw), and Artemus Ward (Charles Farrar Browne). These writers created comic personas through which they presented their personalities and attitudes in wildly exaggerated forms, as Clemens did in his creation of Mark Twain.

His first important literary production was a short sketch entitled 'Jim Smiley and his Jumping Frog' which appeared in a New York newspaper in 1865. The story was reprinted around the country, and it brought its author more than local fame. Four years later Mark Twain had become a national figure; his comic travel letters describing a trip to Europe and the Holy Land were highly successful, and when in 1869 he turned them into a book, *The Innocents Abroad*, it became a best seller— 'It sells right along just like the Bible'. *Roughing It* (1872) continues the comic adventures of Mark Twain; now he is the naïve greenhorn on his first visit to the far West. Clemens was by this time an established writer; he was famous, wealthy, and happily married to Olivia Langdon, whom he adored all his life. In 1873 he collaborated with

3

Charles Dudley Warner to write *The Gilded Age*, an uneven satirical novel that gave a name to the era of speculation and corruption that followed the Civil War.

The most creative phase of Clemens's career began in 1874 when his closest literary friend, William Dean Howells, persuaded him to write a series of articles for the *Atlantic Monthly* commemorating the great days of the Mississippi steamboats. The writing of 'Old Times on the Mississippi' released new imaginative energies that carried him back to his Hannibal boyhood. His next book *The Adventures of Tom Sawyer* (1876) is a celebration of the enchanted world of childhood. When he completed *Tom Sawyer* he immediately began to think about a sequel, and he was also excited by a new narrative method which he explained to Howells in a famous letter written in July, 1875:

I have finished the story & didn't take the chap beyond boyhood. I believe it would be fatal to do it in any shape but autobiographically – like Gil Blas. I perhaps made a mistake in not writing it in the first person. . . . By and by I shall take a boy of twelve & run him on through life (in the first person) but not Tom Sawyer – he would not be a good character for it.

Clemens's narrative experiment resulted in *The Adventures of Huckleberry Finn*. Begun in 1877, but not completed until 1884, *Huckleberry Finn* is more than a book about childhood; it is a book about life seen through a child's eyes, and it describes a world that is at once comic in its absurdities and illusions, and tragic in its violence and cruelty. The central theme of the novel is freedom, and while writing it Clemens discovered an artistic freedom that he could never experience again. In *Huckleberry Finn* he created a unique personality, a new way of looking at the world, and a new language, flexible, incisive and vernacular; a language rich in humour, irony, pity and anger.

The Adventures of Huckleberry Finn stands chronologically almost at the centre of Clemens's career; it marks the fulfilment of his experiments with the comic narrator of his earlier travel books, and it looks forward to the increasing bitterness and disillusion of his later work. *A Connecticut Yankee in King Arthur's Court* (1889) dramatizes the absurdity of human history, in which men are governed by heredity and environment, and the concepts of free-will and progress are illusions. *Pudd'nhead Wilson* (1894) returns to a Missouri village setting, but the humour that characterized *Tom Sawyer* and *Huckleberry Finn* is gone; what remains is a world characterized by slavery, cruelty and deceit. The last twenty-five years of Clemens's career were scarred with sadness; he suffered personal losses and tragedies; his financial speculations ended in bankruptcy, and he was forced to demean his talent by venturing on extensive lecture tours, and by producing second-rate pot-boilers like *The American Claimant* (1892), and *Tom Sawyer Abroad* (1894). His creative imagination turned in old age to places remote in time or space, like the medieval Eseldorf in *The Mysterious Stranger* (1916) where a group of boys are visited by an angelic being who demonstrates to them that human life is utterly meaningless, 'a grotesque and foolish dream'.

In his lifetime Mark Twain achieved a fame and popularity unsurpassed by any American writer, and his reputation is not in the least diminished today. His influence on twentieth-century writing has often been commented upon, notably by T. S. Eliot who saw him as a revolutionary force in English writing:

Twain, at least in *Huckleberry Finn*, reveals himself to be one of those writers of whom there are not a great many in any literature, who have discovered a new way of writing, valid not only for themselves, but for others. I should place him, in this respect, even with Dryden and Swift, as one of those rare writers who have brought their language up to date and in so doing, 'purified the dialect of the tribe'.

When Twain began his career American writing was smothered in the dead rhetoric of the 'genteel tradition'; he stripped away outworn responses and clichés, and replaced them with a fresh, vigorous and, at its best, wonderfully poetic language. As William Dean Howells recognized, Mark Twain was a unique creative force in American literature:

Emerson, Longfellow, Lowell, Holmes—I knew them all and all the rest of sages, poets, seers, critics, humorists; they were like one another and like other literary men; but Clemens was sole, incomparable, the Lincoln of our literature.

Scheme of extracts

The extracts in this book have been chosen in order to illustrate Mark Twain's achievement and development as a writer. Particular attention has been paid to Twain as a humorist and to the central importance of *Huckleberry Finn*. The first section examines Twain's use of the comic narrator—the 'Mark Twain' persona and Huckleberry Finn. Then follows a consideration of a number of Twain's comic techniques, such as burlesque and parody, the tall tale, the dead pan voice and anticlimax. The next section examines Twain's manner of character-portrayal, and is followed by examples illustrating his use of descriptive language. The final section discusses the merging of Twain's humour into the irony and satire of his later works.

Mark Twain was a prolific author who expressed his opinions on many topics and made use of various genres. Much has had to be ignored here, but it is hoped that the examples will provide the reader with an indication of Twain's greatness, and that the bibliography will be consulted when the book fails.

The comic narrator

One of the comic poses which Clemens created for Mark Twain in *The Innocents Abroad* is suggested by the title of the book. In the first chapter we discover Twain in the guise of an impossibly naïve American tourist reading the advertisement for the 'grand' *Quaker City* expedition to Europe and the Holy Land, and apparently being taken in by the inflated rhetoric of the tour organizers. Twain's illusions concerning the advertised 'select' company of the expedition are soon shattered—the promised figures of Rev. Henry Ward Beecher, General Sherman, and the 'Drummer Boy of the Potomac' never materialize, and for the most part the 'pilgrims' are elderly, dull and mealy-mouthed, intent on imposing a regimen of 'solemnity, decorum, dinner, dominoes, devotions and slander' on the voyage. This early anticlimax suggests a basic and recurrent situation in the book, in which the illusions of the naïve narrator about the culture and sophistication of Europe, and the beauty and grandeur of the Holy Land, are systematically stripped away and mocked by actual experience. The first extract illustrates this situation when Mark Twain experiences the barbers of Paris.

I

Then we hunted for a barber-shop. From earliest infancy it had been a cherished ambition of mine to be shaved some day in a palatial barber-shop of Paris. I wished to recline at full length in a cushioned invalid chair, with pictures about me, and sumptuous furniture; with frescoed walls and gilded arches, above me, and vistas of Corinthian columns stretching far before me; with perfumes of Araby to intoxicate my sense, and the slumbrous drone of distant noises to soothe me to sleep. At the end of an hour I would wake up regretfully and find my face as smooth and as soft as an infant's. Departing, I would lift my hands above that barber's head and say, 'Heaven bless you, my son!'

So we searched high and low, for a matter of two hours, but never a barber-shop could we see. We saw only wig-making establishments, with shocks of dead and repulsive hair bound upon the heads of painted waxen brigands who stared out from glass boxes upon the passer-by, with their stony eyes, and scared him with the ghostly white of their countenances. We shunned these signs for a time, but finally we concluded that the wig-makers must of necessity be the barbers as well, since we could find no single legitimate representative of the fraternity. We entered and asked, and found that it was even so.

I said I wanted to be shaved. The barber inquired where my room was. I said, never mind where my room was, I wanted to be shaved—there, on the spot. The doctor said he would be shaved also. Then there was an excitement among those two barbers! There was a wild consultation, and afterwards a hurrying to and fro and a feverish gathering up of razors from obscure places and a ransacking for soap. Next they took us into a little, mean, shabby, back room; they got two ordinary sitting-room chairs and placed us in them, with our coats on.

My old, old dream of bliss vanished into thin air!

I sat bolt upright, silent, sad, and solemn. One of the wig-making outlaws lathered my face for ten uncomfortable minutes and finished by plastering a mass of suds into my mouth. I expelled the unpleasant stuff with a strong English expletive and said, 'Foreigner, beware!' Then this infidel strapped his razor on his boot, hovered over me ominously for six fearful seconds, and then swooped down upon me like the genius of destruction. The first rake of his razor loosened the very hide from my face, and lifted me out of the chair. Let us draw the curtain over this harrowing scene. Suffice it that I submitted, and went through with the cruel infliction of a shave by a French barber; tears of exquisite agony coursed down my cheeks, now and then, but I survived. Then the incipient assassin held a basin of water under my chin and slopped its contents over my face, and into my bosom, and down the back of my neck, with a mean pretence of washing away the soap and blood. He dried my features with a towel, and was going to comb my hair; but I asked to be excused. I said, with scathing irony, that it was sufficient to be skinned—I declined to be scalped.

The Innocents Abroad, vol. 1, ch. 12

Twain prepares for the disaster described in the shaving scene by first building up an image of the fantasy which the burlesque reality outrageously destroys. Clichés of romantic travel are used to elaborate the fantasy—'vistas of Corinthian columns', 'perfumes of Araby'—and the whole experience is envisaged by Twain as a sensuous and exotic indulgence. The destruction of this absurd romantic dream follows in stages. First, the travellers cannot identify their dream palace, discovering only wig shops with 'shocks of dead and repulsive hair bound upon the heads of painted waxen brigands'. Notice how the window display points ironically forward to the mock murder that follows. When Twain finally encounters the barber 'villains' in their 'shabby back room' they are the complete antithesis of his romantic fantasy, and the dream of exotic luxury is replaced by a farcical and painful reality in which the barber fills his victim's mouth with soap, rakes the skin from his face, and completes the operation by throwing water over him. The naïve traveller discovers in Paris conditions reminiscent of the American frontier—(the barber strops his razor on his boot!). The happenings and sensations are all filtered through the memory of the narrator, and he records them with a matter of fact directness and irony that preclude self-pity: the joke he tells is directed against himself.

Mark Twain in *The Innocents Abroad* is far from being a static figure, and as the narrative progresses he takes on various, sometimes conflicting, comic roles. At times he masquerades as the genteel man of letters that Clemens himself half-wished to be; he spouts the romantic rhetoric of nineteenth-century travel books when faced with the 'sublimities' of Europe and the Holy Land, only to mock himself on the next page. (See, for example, his description of the Sea of Galilee, *The Innocents Abroad*, vol. 11, ch. 21.) He also presents himself as a cynical realist who refuses to be intimidated by respectable, genteel viewpoints, which he mocks in the light of his own experience. Here, for example, is his unique response to Leonardo da Vinci's painting of 'The Last Supper'.

2

Here, in Milan, in an ancient tumble-down ruin of a church, is the mournful wreck of the most celebrated painting in the world—'The Last Supper,' by Leonardo da Vinci. We are not infallible judges of pictures, but of course we went there to see this wonderful painting, once so beautiful, always so worshipped by masters in art, and for ever to be famous in song and story. And the first thing that occurred was the infliction on us of a placard fairly reeking in wretched English. Take a morsel of it:

'Bartholomew (that is the first figure on the left hand side at the spectator), uncertain and doubtful about what he thinks to have heard, and upon which he wants to be assured by himself at Christ and by no others.'

Good, isn't it? And then Peter is described as 'argumenting in a threatening and angrily condition at Judas Iscariot.'

This paragraph recalls the picture. The Last Supper is painted on the dilapidated wall of what was a little chapel attached to the main church in ancient times; I suppose. It is battered and scarred in every direction, and stained and discoloured by time, and Napoleon's horses kicked the legs off most of the disciples when they (the horses, not the disciples) were stabled there more than half a century ago. ...

This picture is about thirty feet long and ten or twelve high, I should think, and the figures are at least life-size. It is one of the largest paintings in Europe.

The colors are dimmed with age; the countenances are scaled and marred, and nearly all expression is gone from them; the hair is a dead blur upon the wall, and there is no life in the eyes. Only the attitudes are certain.

People come here from all parts of the world and glorify this masterpiece. They stand entranced before it with bated breath and parted lips, and when they speak, it is only in the catchy ejaculations of rapture:

'Oh, wonderful!'
'Such expression!'
'Such grace of attitude!'
'Such dignity!'
'Such faultless drawing!'

'Such matchless coloring!'
'Such feeling!'
'What delicacy of touch!'
'What sublimity of conception!'
'A vision! A vision!'

I only envy these people; I envy them their honest admiration, if it be honest—their delight, if they feel delight. I harbor no animosity toward any of them. But at the same time the thought *will* intrude itself upon me: How can they see what is not visible?

The Innocents Abroad, vol. 1, ch. 19

Twain's reaction to 'The Last Supper', despite his apparent casualness, is skilfully presented. He prepares us for his unorthodox response to the painting by first describing its surrounding. He begins with the ruined church which houses it, moves on to the ruined language of the 'official' description, then to the dilapidated wall on which it is painted, before finally arriving at the ruined painting. The total effect he builds up is one of decrepitude. The one positive feature of the painting that he mentions is its size—a deliberately non-aesthetic consideration. In fact Twain carefully avoids coming to terms with the painting's artistic merits; his viewpoint is narrow and naturalistic, and he describes the painting as if it were a weather worn bill-board. Comedy arises from the enormous discrepancy between what Twain had been led to believe existed by 'good authorities', and what he insists he saw there. The narrator's attitude is mocking, philistine, even arrogant; but it is his own, and his determination to see for himself is balanced against the nonsense of the 'official' description, and the clichés of the stock learned responses which are allowed to speak for themselves.

After describing his comic pilgrimage to Europe and the Holy Land in *The Innocents Abroad*, Mark Twain stepped backwards in time, choosing for the subject of *Roughing It* his experiences as a young man in the American West. Once again Mark Twain's naïvety is deliberately exaggerated for the purposes of comedy. In the following extract he has arrived in Carson City, Nevada, where he becomes stricken with envy on seeing the romantic-looking professional cow-boys cavorting through the streets of the town.

3

I resolved to have a horse to ride. I had never seen such wild, free, magnificent horsemanship outside of a circus as these picturesquely clad Mexicans, Californians, and Mexicanized Americans displayed in Carson streets every day. How they rode! Leaning just gently forward out of the perpendicular, easy and nonchalant, with broad slouch-hat brim blown square up in front, and long riata swinging above the head, they swept through the town like the wind! The next minute they were only a sailing puff of dust on the far desert. If they trotted, they sat up gallantly and gracefully, and seemed part of the horse; did not go jiggering up and down after the silly Miss-Nancy fashion of the riding-schools. I had quickly learned to tell a horse from a cow, and was full of anxiety to learn more. I was resolved to buy a horse.

Roughing It, vol. i, ch. 24

Mark Twain's ambition to own a horse is realized when he witnesses an impromptu street auction at which a particularly ungainly looking animal is being sold. While he wistfully watches the proceedings, he is approached by an apparently friendly stranger who assures the naïve greenhorn that the animal he sees before him is not an ordinary horse, but a 'Genuine Mexican Plug'.

4

A man whom I did not know (he turned out to be the auctioneer's brother) noticed the wistful look in my eye, and observed that that was a very remarkable horse to be going at such a price; and added that the saddle alone was worth the money. It was a Spanish saddle, with ponderous *tapidaros*, and furnished with the ungainly sole-leather covering with the unspellable name. I said I had half a notion to bid. Then this keen-eyed person appeared to me to be 'taking my measure'; but I dismissed the suspicion when he spoke, for his manner was full of guileless candor and truthfulness. Said he:

'I know that horse—know him well. You are a stranger, I take it, and so you might think he was an American horse, maybe, but I assure you he is not. He is nothing of the kind; but—excuse my speaking in a low voice, other people being near—he is, without the shadow of a doubt, a Genuine Mexican Plug!'

I did not know what a Genuine Mexican Plug was, but there was something about this man's way of saying it that made me swear inwardly that I would own a Genuine Mexican Plug, or die.

'Has he any other—er—advantages?' I inquired, suppressing what eagerness I could.

He hooked his forefinger in the pocket of my army shirt, led me to one side, and breathed in my ear impressively these words:

'He can outbuck anything in America!'

'Going, going, going—at *twent-ty* four dollars and a half, gen—'

'Twenty-seven!' I shouted, in a frenzy.

'And sold!' said the auctioneer, and passed over the Genuine Mexican Plug to me.

I could scarcely contain my exultation. I paid the money, and put the animal in a neighboring livery stable to dine and rest himself.

In the afternoon I brought the creature into the plaza, and certain citizens held him by the head, and others by the tail, while I mounted him. As soon as they let go, he placed all his feet in a bunch together, lowered his back, and then suddenly arched it upward, and shot me straight into the air a matter of three or four feet! I came as straight down again, lit in the saddle, went instantly up again, came down almost on the high pommel, shot up again, and came down on the horse's neck—all in the space of three or four seconds. Then he rose and stood almost straight up on his hind feet, and I, clasping his lean neck desperately, slid back into the saddle, and held on. He came down, and immediately hoisted his heels into the air, delivering a vicious kick at the sky, and stood on his forefeet. And then down he came once more, and began the original exercise of shooting me straight up again. The third time I went up I heard a stranger say:

'Oh, *don't* he buck, though!'

I sat down on a stone, with a sigh, and by a natural impulse one of my hands sought my forehead, and the other the base of my stomach. I believe I never appreciated, till then, the poverty of the human machinery—for I still needed a hand or two to place elsewhere. Pen cannot describe how I was jolted up. Imagination cannot conceive how disjointed I was—how, internally, externally, and universally I was unsettled, mixed up, and ruptured. There was a sympathetic crowd around me, though.

One elderly-looking comforter said:

'Stranger, you've been taken in. Everybody in this camp knows that horse. Any child, any Injun, could have told you that he'd buck; he is the very worst devil to buck on the continent of America. You hear *me*. I'm Curry. *Old* Curry. Old *Abe* Curry. And moreover, he is a simon-pure, out-and-out, genuine d—d Mexican plug, and an uncommon mean one at that, too. Why, you turnip, if you had laid low and kept dark, there's chances to buy an *American* horse for mighty little more than you paid for that bloody old foreign relic.'

I gave no sign; but I made up my mind that if the auctioneer's brother's funeral took place while I was in the Territory I would postpone all other recreations and attend it.

Roughing It, vol. 1, ch. 24

The comedy in this siuation arises out of the narrator's ability to remember his own greenhorn days, and to expose and laugh at his former ignorance and vanity. Notice the strategy by which the stranger persuades Mark Twain to buy the horse—he tells him the truth about it! He ironically draws Twain into the deal by telling him about the horse's drawbacks, making them sound like virtues, and then relying on his intuitive knowledge of the greenhorn's ignorance and vanity to do the rest. The sale is, of course, a clever trick arranged by the auctioneer and his brother. But doesn't the success of the trick depend on the characters of the participants? Mark Twain's exposure as a greenhorn is all the more effective because he brings it upon himself; his pride leads him to perform in the public square before a crowd of amused onlookers. But what could have been a cruel situation is turned into comedy by Twain's response to it. Instead of resorting to the destructive emotions of anger or self-pity, he takes cover in humour. He joins in the mockery of the onlookers, and laughs at his own humiliation by exaggerating it into unreality: 'Pen cannot describe ... Imagination cannot conceive ...' Even Twain's feelings of revenge against the auctioneer's brother are transformed into comedy at the end when he imagines himself getting his own back at the man's funeral. Notice also the part played by the crowd in this archetypal situation in American humour. They are amused at the spectacle Twain has made of himself, but at the same time they are sympathetic and friendly, anxious that he should learn from his experience. Mark Twain here takes part in a form of ceremony of initiation similar to that experienced by Robin in Hawthorne's story 'My Kinsman Major Molineux', in which the greenhorn loses his innocence and joins in the laughter of the old-timers with whom he henceforth identifies himself.

A similar tension between Mark Twain, the callow and naïve young man, and Mark Twain, the experienced old-timer looking back on his greenhorn days, is evident in the next extract which is taken from *Life on the Mississippi*. Here Mark Twain is an immature young 'cub' pilot on the Mississippi, vain and complacent in his unfounded belief that he had learned to navigate the river. His master-pilot and teacher, Mr. Bixby, arranges for the puffed-up 'cub' to be deflated and brought back to reality.

5

Mr. Bixby said—

'I am going below a while. I suppose you know the next crossing?'

This was almost an affront. It was about the plainest and simplest crossing in the whole river. One couldn't come to any harm, whether he ran it right or not; and as for depth, there never had been any bottom there. I knew all this, perfectly well.

'Know how to *run* it? Why, I can run it with my eyes shut.'

'How much water is there in it?'

'Well, that is an odd question. I couldn't get bottom there with a church steeple.'

'You think so, do you?'

The very tone of the question shook my confidence. That was what Mr. Bixby was expecting. He left, without saying anything more. I began to imagine all sorts of things. Mr. Bixby, unknown to me, of course, sent somebody down to the forecastle with some mysterious instruction to the leadsmen, another messenger was sent to whisper among the officers, and then Mr. Bixby went into hiding behind a smoke stack where he could observe results. Presently the captain stepped out on the hurricane deck; next the chief mate appeared; then a clerk. Every moment or two a straggler was added to my audience; and before I got to the head of the island I had fifteen or twenty people assembled down there under my nose. I began to wonder what the trouble was. As I started across, the captain glanced aloft at me and said with a sham uneasiness in his voice—

'Where is Mr. Bixby?'

'Gone below, sir.'

But that did the business for me. My imagination began to construct dangers out of nothing, and they multiplied faster than I could keep the run of them. All at once I imagined I saw shoal water ahead! The wave of coward agony that surged through me then came near dislocating every joint in me. All my confidence in that crossing vanished. I seized the bell rope; dropped it, ashamed; seized it again; dropped it once more; clutched it tremblingly once again, and pulled it so feebly that I could hardly hear the stroke myself. Captain and mate sang out instantly, and both together—

'Starboard lead there! And quick about it!'

This was another shock. I began to climb the wheel like a squirrel; but I would hardly get the boat started to port before I would see new dangers on that side, and away I would spin to the other; only to find perils accumulating to starboard, and be crazy to get to port again. Then came the leadsman's sepulchral cry:

'D-e-e-p four!'

Deep four in a bottomless crossing! The terror of it took my breath away.

'M-a-r-k three! ... M-a-r-k three ... Quarter less three! ... Half twain!'

This was frightful! I seized the bell ropes and stopped the engines.

'Quarter twain! Quarter twain! *Mark* twain!'

I was helpless. I did not know what in the world to do. I was quaking from head to foot, and I could have hung my hat on my eyes, they stuck out so far.

'Quarter *less* twain! Nine and a *half!*'

We were *drawing* nine! My hands were in a nerveless flutter. I could not ring a bell intelligibly with them. I flew to the speaking tube and shouted to the engineer—

'Oh, Ben, if you love me, *back* her! Quick, Ben! Oh, back the immortal *soul* out of her!'

I heard the door close gently. I looked around, and there stood Mr. Bixby, smiling a bland, sweet smile. Then the audience on the hurricane deck sent up a thundergust of humiliating laughter. I saw it all, now, and I felt meaner than the meanest man in human history. I laid in the lead, set the boat in her marks, came ahead on the engines, and said:

'It was a fine trick to play on an orphan, *wasn't* it? I suppose I'll never hear the last of how I was ass enough to heave the lead at the head of 66.'

'Well, no, you won't, maybe. In fact I hope you won't; for I want you to learn something by that experience. Didn't you *know* there was no bottom in that crossing?'

'Yes, sir, I did.'

'Very well, then. You shouldn't have allowed me or anybody else to shake your confidence in that knowledge. Try to remember that. And another thing: when you get into a dangerous place, don't turn coward. That isn't going to help matters any.'

It was a good enough lesson, but pretty hardly learned. Yet about the hardest part of it was that for months I so often had to hear a phrase which I had conceived a particular distaste for. It was, 'Oh, Ben, if you love me, back her!'

Life on the Mississippi, ch. 13

Like the previous extract from *Roughing It*, this passage describes a humiliating experience for Mark Twain, in which his imperfections, character and knowledge are exposed before an amused and experienced audience whom he had intended to impress with his maturity and ability. But the situation here is rather more complex. In *Roughing It* Mark Twain was the dupe in the horse-trading story, but now he is responsible for the safety of a steamboat, and his inadequacies could endanger the lives of crew and passengers.

The cub's complacent vanity which is evident in his smug facetiousness, is an illusion of self-reliance, and as soon as he is alone he becomes irresolute and panic-stricken. The tension in the passage is built up with the boy's accelerating panic. There is an absence of elaborate language and metaphor, the sentences are short and direct, and verbs of action proliferate. The comedy here is noticeably less farcical than in previous extracts; it depends for its success more on character than on accidental situations. Does not the action in the passage depend both on Mr. Bixby's shrewdness and Mark Twain's vanity and cowardice? There is also recognition here of the moral basis of comedy that looks forward to *Huckleberry Finn*; as Mr. Bixby points out, the ceremony of humiliation has an intended moral purpose: 'I want you to learn something by that experience.' And, despite his momentary lapse into self-pity (the orphan reference), Twain does recognize that his comic humiliation has been necessary: 'It was a good enough lesson but pretty hardly learned.'

Life on the Mississippi is the last important book in which Mark Twain appears as a comic character. The later travel books, *A Tramp Abroad* and *Following the Equator*, are narrated by Mark Twain, but despite occasional scenes of comic brilliance they are disappointing works. They give the impression of a tired author content to write travelogues, and the comic figure of Mark Twain becomes submerged in the identity of a more 'serious' and more mundane Samuel Clemens. The true descendant of the Mark Twain of *The Innocents Abroad*, *Roughing It*, and *Life on the Mississippi* is Huckleberry Finn; he inherits Twain's perception and his unique way of looking at the world.

6

Well, all through the circus they done the most astonishing things; and all the time that clown carried on so it most killed the people. The ringmaster couldn't even say a word to him but he was back at him quick as a wink with the funniest things a body ever said; and how he ever *could* think of so many of them, and so sudden and so pat, was what I couldn't no way understand. Why, I couldn't 'a' thought of them in a year. And by and by a drunken man tried to get into the ring—said he wanted to ride; said he could ride as well as anybody that ever was. They argued and tried to keep him out, but he wouldn't listen, and the whole show come to a standstill. Then the people begun to holler at him and make fun of him, and that made him mad, and he begun to rip and tear; so that stirred up the people, and a lot of men begun to pile down off of the benches and swarm toward the ring, saying, 'Knock him down! throw him out!' and one or two women begun to scream. So, then, the ringmaster he made a little speech, and said he hoped there wouldn't be no disturbance, and if the man would promise he wouldn't make no more trouble he would let him ride if he thought he could stay on the horse. So everybody laughed and said all right, and the man got on. The minute he was on, the horse begun to rip and tear and jump and cavort around, with two circus men hanging on to his bridle trying to hold him, and the drunken man hanging on to his neck, and his heels flying in the air every jump, and the whole crowd of people standing up shouting and laughing till tears rolled down. And at last, sure enough, all the circus men could do, the horse broke loose, and away he went like the very nation, round and round the ring, with that sot laying down on him and hanging to his neck, with first one leg hanging most to the ground on one side, and then t'other one on t'other side, and the people just crazy. It warn't funny to me, though; I was all of a tremble to see his danger. But pretty soon he struggled up astraddle and grabbed the bridle, a-reeling this way and that; and the next minute he sprung up and dropped the bridle and stood! and the horse a-going like a house afire, too. He just stood up there, a-sailing around as easy and comfortable as if he warn't ever drunk in his life—and then he began to pull off his clothes and sling them. He shed them so thick they kind of clogged up the air, and altogether he shed seventeen suits. And, then, there he was, slim and handsome, and dressed the gaudiest and prettiest you ever saw, and he lit into that horse with his whip and made him fairly hum— and finally skipped off, and made his bow and danced off to the dressing-room, and everybody just a-howling with pleasure and astonishment.

Then the ringmaster he see how he had been fooled, and he *was* the sickest ringmaster you ever see, I reckon. Why, it was one of his own men! He had got up that joke all out of his own head, and never let on to nobody. Well, I felt sheepish enough to be took in so, but I wouldn't 'a' been in that ringmaster's place, not for a thousand dollars. I don't know; there may be bullier circuses than what that one was, but I never struck them yet. Anyways, it was plenty good enough for *me*; and wherever I run across it, it can have all of *my* custom every time.

Huckleberry Finn, ch. 22

23

One of the qualities that Huck inherits from the Mark Twain persona is his naïvety; he is willing to accept experience at face value be it Tom Sawyer's romantic lies, Miss Watson's religion, the Grangerfords' 'civilization', or the madly absurd identities of the King and the Duke. When their falsity is experienced and revealed to him the effect is both disturbing and comic. In this episode Huck is quite prepared to accept the genuineness of the circus rider, and even when he realizes that the rider is a circus clown, he does not understand the full dimensions of the trick, which he sees being played on the ringmaster rather than on himself. Like Mark Twain in Europe and the Far West, Huck lives in a world made up of shifting illusions; a world like that of the circus clown who peels away layer after layer, and all that is left in the end is but another deception. Is it not possible to see this episode as a microcosm not only of the world of Huckleberry Finn, but of the world of Mark Twain's fiction as a whole? The only hope Huck has of penetrating the layers of deception and illusion around him is to rely on his unique pragmatic perception of things; this is the lesson Mr. Bixby had attempted to teach Mark Twain on the river.

Even from the small evidence of this extract it is clear that the character of Huck Finn is richer and more complex than that of the Mark Twain figure. He is not simply a one-dimensional comic figure as Twain often is; we see here Huck's naïvety, but also his wonder, excitement, admiration and pity: 'It warn't funny to me, though; I was all of a tremble to see his danger.' With the creation of Huckleberry Finn, Clemens extended his vision beyond the boundaries of Mark Twain.

Techniques of humour

One of the most characteristic devices of Western oral humour is the use of the dead-pan expression, a solemn poker face that recites absurdities and wild exaggerations, while at the same time betraying no sense that anything humorous could be intended. It is a device that Clemens made famous on the lecture platform in his characterization of Mark Twain, with his mock serious expression of innocence, and slow, careful drawl. Clemens later described this technique as the basis of the American art of humorous story telling:

The humorous story is told gravely; the teller does his best to conceal the fact that he even dimly suspects that there is anything funny about it; ... To string incongruities and absurdities together in a wandering and sometimes purposeless way and seem innocently unaware that they are absurdities, is the basis of the American art, if my position is correct.

This is a precise description of the style of humour adopted by Simon Wheeler in 'The Celebrated Jumping Frog of Calaveras County'. Mark Twain, in the guise of an aloof gentleman, goes 'at the request of a friend of mine who wrote me from the East' to a decayed mining camp in Nevada in order to enquire after a mythical character who goes under the unlikely name of Rev. Leonidas W. Smiley. Here he meets Simon Wheeler, an old bar-room loafer.

7

I found Simon Wheeler dozing comfortably by the bar-room stove of the old, dilapidated tavern in the ancient mining camp of Angel's, and I noticed that he was fat and bald-headed, and had an expression of winning gentleness and simplicity upon his tranquil countenance. He roused up and gave me good-day. I told him a friend of mine had commissioned me to make some inquiries about a cherished companion of his boyhood named *Leonidas W. Smiley—Rev. Leonidas W.* Smiley—a young minister of the Gospel, who he had heard was at one time a resident of Angel's Camp. I added that, if Mr. Wheeler could tell me anything about this Rev. Leonidas W. Smiley, I would feel under many obligations to him.

Simon Wheeler backed me into a corner and blockaded me there with this chair, and then sat me down and reeled off the monotonous narrative which follows this paragraph. He never smiled, he never frowned, he never changed his voice from the gentle-flowing key to which he tuned the initial sentence, he never betrayed the slightest suspicion of enthusiasm; but all through the interminable narrative there ran a vein of impressive earnestness and sincerity, which showed me plainly that, so far from his imagining that there was anything ridiculous or funny about his story, he regarded it as a really important matter, and admired its two heroes as men of transcendent genius in finesse. To me, the spectacle of a man drifting serenely along through such a queer yarn without ever smiling, was exquisitely absurd. As I said before, I asked him to tell me what he knew of Rev. Leonidas W. Smiley,

and he replied as follows. I let him go on in his own way, and never interrupted him once.
'The Celebrated Jumping Frog of Calaveras County'

Mark Twain presents himself here as a genteel visitor to the West who sees Simon Wheeler as a genial country bumpkin. His supercilious and patronizing attitude is reflected in the way he speaks to the reader. With his ostentatious formality, ('I would feel under many obligations'), and his pretentious artificial style, ('tranquil countenance', 'cherished companion'), Mark Twain cannot penetrate the vernacular mask of Simon Wheeler. He is the archetypal genteel visitor to the West duped by appearances, and if Simon appears as a seedy bumpkin, it is only because we are limited to Twain's viewpoint; and it is this viewpoint that is mocked by Simon's ensuing dead-pan monologue. Twain's enquiry about the mythical Leonidas W. Smiley is Simon's cue to launch into an inconclusive harangue on a local gambler by the name of Jim Smiley who bet on everything and anything. Jim Smiley owned an old mare known as the 'fifteen-minute nag' who always appeared to be dying, yet defeated appearances by coming from behind to win her races. Jim also owned an equally remarkable bull terrier named 'Andrew Jackson' who incapacitated his opponents in dog-fights by holding on to their hind legs! But Jim's greatest source of pride was his wonderful jumping frog, 'Dan'l Webster', and it is the story of the outwitting of Jim Smiley and his pretentious frog that is the climax and moral centre of Simon Wheeler's dead-pan monologue.

8

Well, Smiley kep' the beast in a little lattice box, and

he used to fetch him down-town sometimes and lay for a bet. One day a feller—a stranger in the camp, he was—come acrost him with his box and says:

'What might it be that you've got in the box?'

And Smiley says, sorter indifferent-like, 'It might be a parrot, or it might be a canary, maybe, but it ain't—it's only just a frog.'

And the feller took it and looked at it careful, and turned it round this way and that, and says, 'H'm—so 'tis. Well, what's *he* good for?'

'Well,' Smiley says, easy and careless, 'he's good enough for *one* thing, I should judge—he can outjump any frog in Calaveras County.'

The feller took the box again, and took another long, particular look, and give it back to Smiley and says, very deliberate, 'Well,' he says, 'I don't see no p'ints about that frog that's any better'n any other frog.'

'Maybe you don't,' Smiley says. 'Maybe you understand frogs, and maybe you don't understand 'em; maybe you've had experience, and maybe you ain't only a amature, as it were. Anyways, I've got *my* opinion, and I'll resk forty dollars that he can outjump any frog in Calaveras County.'

And the feller studied a minute, and then says, kinder sad like, 'Well, I'm only a stranger here, and I an't got no frog; but if I had a frog, I'd bet you.'

And then Smiley says, 'That's all right—that's all right—if you'll hold my box a minute, I'll go and get you a frog.' And so the feller took the box, and put up his forty dollars along with Smiley's and set down to wait.

So he set there a good while thinking and thinking to hisself, and then he got the frog out and prized his mouth open and took a teaspoon and filled him full of quail shot—filled him pretty near up to his chin—and set him on the floor. Smiley he went to the swamp and slopped around in the mud for a long time, and finally

28

he ketched a frog, and fetched him in, and give him to this feller, and says:

'Now, if you're ready, set him alongside of Dan'l, with his fore-paws just even with Dan'l, and I'll give the word.' Then he says, 'One—two—three—jump!' and him and the feller touched up the frogs from behind, and the new frog hopped off, but Dan'l give a heave, and hysted up his shoulders—so—like a Frenchman, but it wasn't no use—it couldn't budge; he was planted as solid as an anvil, and he couldn't no more stir than if he was anchored out. Smiley was a good deal surprised, and he was disgusted too, but he didn't have no idea what the matter was, of course.

The feller took the money and started away; and when he was going out at the door, he sorter jerked his thumb over his shoulders—this way—at Dan'l, and says again, very deliberate, 'Well, *I* don't see no p'ints about that frog that's any better'n any other frog.'

Smiley he stood scratching his head and looking down at Dan'l a long time, and at last he says, 'I do wonder what in the nation that frog throw'd off for—I wonder if there ain't something the matter with him—he 'pears to look mighty baggy, somehow.' And he ketched Dan'l by the nap of the neck, and lifted him up and says, 'Why, blame my cats, if he don't weight five pound!' and turned him upside down, and he belched out a double handful of shot. And then he see how it was, and he was the maddest man—he set the frog down and took out after that feller, but he never ketched him. And—

[Here Simon Wheeler heard his name called from the front yard, and got up to see what was wanted.] And turning to me as he moved away, he said: 'Just set where you are, stranger, and rest easy—I an't going to be gone a second.'

But, by your leave, I did not think that a continuation of the history of the enterprising vagabond *Jim* Smiley would be likely to afford me much information concerning the Rev. *Leonidas W*. Smiley, and so I started away.

At the door I met the sociable Wheeler returning, and he buttonholed me and recommenced:

'Well, thish-yer Smiley had a yaller one-eyed cow that didn't have no tail, only jest a short stump like a bannanner, and—'

'Oh! hang Smiley and his afflicted cow!' I muttered, good-naturedly, and bidding the old gentleman good-day, I departed.

'The Celebrated Jumping Frog of Calaveras County'

The story of 'Dan'l Webster' like that of 'Andrew Jackson' and the 'fifteen-minute' nag is one of upset expectations; so is Mark Twain's encounter with Simon Wheeler. Where he led us to expect a simple yokel we find a sophisticated humorist whose mask of innocence takes in the genteel visitor and exposes his pretentiousness. Simon's apparently irrelevant narrative is, of course, a carefully sustained exposition of his own relationship with Mark Twain. Is it being too pretentious to see the story as one of cultural antagonisms, centring around contrasting ways of speaking and looking at the world? Notice how the stranger leads Jim Smiley on into the competition but never betrays his strategy; so Simon never betrays his, but leaves Twain to discover for himself how he has been taken in.

Parody and Burlesque

The dead-pan expression is also evident in the next extract taken from *The Innocents Abroad* where Mark Twain presents himself as a grief-stricken traveller who has just discovered the tomb of an ancestor—Adam! Twain's poker-faced solemnity on this occasion adds to, but does not disguise, the burlesque experience he relates:

9

If even greater proofs than those I have mentioned are
wanted, to satisfy the headstrong and the foolish that this
is the genuine center of the earth, they are here. The
greatest of them lies in the fact that from under this very
column was taken the *dust from which Adam was made.*
This can surely be regarded in the light of a settler. It is not
likely that the original first man would have been made
from an inferior quality of earth when it was entirely
convenient to get first quality from the world's center.
This will strike any reflecting mind forcibly. That Adam
was formed of dirt procured in this very spot is amply
proven by the fact that in six thousand years no man
has ever been able to prove that the dirt was *not* procured here whereof he was made.

It is a singular circumstance that right under the roof of
this same great church, and not far away from that illus-
trious column, Adam himself, the father of the human
race, lies buried. There is no question that he is actually
buried in the grave which is pointed out as his—there
can be none—because it has never yet been proven that
that grave is not the grave in which he is buried.

The tomb of Adam! How touching it was, here in a
land of strangers, far away from home and friends and
all who cared for me, thus to discover the grave of a
blood relation. True, a distant one, but still a relation.
The unerring instinct of nature thrilled its recognition.
The fountain of my filial affection was stirred to its pro-
foundest depths, and I gave way to tumultuous emotion.
I leaned upon a pillar and burst into tears. I deem it no
shame to have wept over the grave of my poor dead
relative. Let him who would sneer at my emotion close
this volume here, for he will find little to his taste in my

journeyings through Holy Land. Noble old man—he did not live to see me—he did not live to see his child. And I—I—alas, I did not live to see him. Weighed down by sorrow and disappointment, he died before I was born—six thousand brief summers before I was born. But let us try to bear it with fortitude. Let us trust that he is better off where he is. Let us take comfort in the thought that his loss is our eternal gain.

The Innocents Abroad, vol. II, ch. 26

Burlesque and parody are forms that often merge into each other. Burlesque can be defined as the mocking of a subject by incongruous imitation, whereas parody is a more restricted literary humour which mocks a style by applying it to trivial or discordant materials. Both forms of humour depend on an original 'serious' subject or style to deride by ridiculous imitation. In this instance Mark Twain's ostentatious mourning at the Tomb of Adam is a parody of William C. Prime's dithyramb over Jerusalem in *Tent Life in the Holy Land*, a book that especially infuriated Clemens because of its sentimentality, lies and cheap emotional rhetoric. But in this extract the humour hints at more than simple burlesque of a now forgotten Victorian travel book. For the purposes of comedy Twain briefly assumes a new identity; he becomes one of the 'pilgrims', those conventional, self-righteous fools who swallow and revel in the preposterous 'official line' put out by William C. Prime and other 'authorities'. The first two paragraphs are a burlesque of the 'pilgrims'' way of thinking, which is revealed as illogical, self-involved, and utterly complacent. Their emotional indulgence is exaggerated into grotesque proportions, and mocked by the pompous cliché-ridden language Twain resorts to when faced with his momentous discovery—'fountain of my filial affection', 'unerring instinct of nature'. This

32

imaginary Tomb of Adam is discovered by Twain in the Church of the Holy Sepulchre in Jerusalem, the ultimate destination of the pious pilgrimage, and, we are assured, the centre of the world! Yet Twain is surely right to affirm that this burlesque tomb lies at the centre of the world, for the world of his fiction is based on an impulse to laugh at the absurdities of human nature.

Against the 'pilgrims' of *The Innocents Abroad* are set the 'sinners', the 'boys'—Jack, Dan, Moult and, of course, Mark Twain, who are intent on seeing things honestly and for themselves, and on having a good time in the process. The conflict between the 'pilgrims' and the 'sinners' which goes on throughout the book, is prepared for when the 'boys' visit the Paris Zoo and encounter the 'Pilgrim' bird.

10

In the great Zoological Gardens, we found specimens of all the animals the world produces, I think, including a dromedary, a monkey ornamented with tufts of brilliant blue and carmine hair—a very gorgeous monkey he was —a hippopotamus from the Nile, and a sort of tall, long-legged bird with a beak like a powderhorn, and close-fitting wings like the tails of a dress coat. This fellow stood up with his eyes shut and his shoulders stooped forward a little, and looked as if he had his hands under his coat tails. Such tranquil stupidity, such supernatural gravity, such self-righteousness, and such ineffable self-complacency as were in the countenance and attitude of that grey-bodied, dark-winged, bald-headed, and pre-posterously uncomely bird! He was so ungainly, so pimply about the head, so scaly about the legs; yet so serene, so unspeakably satisfied! He was the most comical looking creature that can be imagined. It was good to hear Dan and the doctor laugh—such natural and such

33

enjoyable laughter had not been heard among our excursionists since our ship sailed away from America. This bird was a god-send to us, and I should be an ingrate if I forgot to make honourable mention of him in these pages. Ours was a pleasure excursion; therefore we stayed with that bird an hour, and made the most of him. We stirred him up occasionally, but he only unclosed an eye and slowly closed it again, abating no jot of his stately piety of demeanour or his tremendous seriousness. He only seemed to say: 'Defile not Heaven's anointed with unsanctified hands.' We did not know his name, and so we called him 'The Pilgrim.' Dan said:

'All he wants now is a Plymouth Collection.'

The Innocents Abroad, vol. 1, ch. 11

The sight of the preposterous 'Pilgrim' bird offers to Mark Twain and his companions a heaven-sent symbol which sums up and ridicules the physical and mental characteristics of the 'pilgrims'. What is most striking about this bird is its ugliness, its silly self-righteous appearance, and its complacency; its composure is not even ruffled when it is 'stirred up' by the boys. This episode prepares for the ensuing relationship between the two groups—the 'sinners' continually strive to provoke the 'pilgrims' out of their complacency, but with no success. The 'pilgrims' are mocked here by being lumped together and reduced to the image of a grotesque-looking bird, who has not the sense or imagination to respond to their provocations other than by repeating foolish defensive clichés.

The Tall Story

An important element in Clemens's art is the tall story, a technique of comedy popular in America since Colonial times. The classic movement of the tall story describes adventures which rise by degrees from a mundane, matter of fact level, to a plane of wild fantasy. The hero's incredible physical feats were matched in stories like T. B. Thorpe's 'The Big Bear of Arkansas' (1841) by a linguistic virtuosity; he celebrated his adventures in a vigorous colloquial idiom. The best examples of Mark Twain's use of the tall story are to be found in *Roughing It*, itself an elaborate tall tale about Mark Twain's career in the far West. In the next extract the stage coach carrying Twain to Nevada has broken down on the Prairies. The passengers divert themselves by conducting a buffalo hunt which ends in disaster for a man named Bemis who is chased by a bull buffalo, and has to take refuge in a tree. For a while afterwards he is sullen and withdrawn; then he begins to 'soften up' and he tells the assembled passengers the tall story of his recent adventure.

11

Then the bull came charging at us, and my horse dropped down on all fours and took a fresh start—and then for the next ten minutes he would actually throw one handspring after another so fast that the bull began to get unsettled, too, and didn't know where to start in—and so he stood there sneezing, and shoveling dust over his back, and bellowing every now and then, and thinking he had got a fifteen-hundred-dollar circus horse for breakfast, certain. Well, I was first out on his neck—the horse's, not the bull's—and then underneath, and next on his rump, and sometimes head up, and sometimes heels— but I tell you it seemed solemn and awful to be ripping and tearing and carrying on so in the presence of death, as you might say. Pretty soon the bull made a snatch for us and brought away some of my horse's tail (I suppose, but do not know, being pretty busy at the time), but

35

something made him hungry for solitude and suggested to him to get up and hunt for it. And then you ought to have seen that spider-legged old skeleton go! And you ought to have seen the bull cut out after him, too—head down, tongue out, tail up, bellowing like everything, and actually mowing down the weeds, and tearing up the earth, and boosting up the sand like a whirlwind! By George, it was a hot race! I and the saddle were back on the rump, and I had the bridle in my teeth and holding onto the pommel with both hands. First we left the dogs behind; then we passed a jackass rabbit; then we overtook a coyote, and were gaining on an antelope when the rotten girth let go and threw me about thirty yards off to the left, and as the saddle went down over the horse's rump he gave it a lift with his heels that sent it more than four hundred yards up in the air, I wish I may die in a minute if he didn't. I fell at the foot of the only solitary tree there was in nine counties adjacent (as any creature could see with the naked eye), and the next second I had hold of the bark with four sets of nails and my teeth, and the next second after that I was astraddle of the main limb and blaspheming my luck in a way that made my breath smell of brimstone. I *had* the bull now, if he did not think of *one* thing. But that one thing I dreaded. I dreaded it very seriously. There was a possibility that the bull might not think of it, but there were greater chances that he would. I made up my mind what I would do in case he did. It was a little over forty feet to the ground from where I sat. I cautiously unwound the lariat from the pommel of my saddle—'

'Your *saddle?* Did you take your saddle up in the tree with you?'

'Take it up in the tree with me? Why, how you talk. Of course I didn't. No man could do that. It *fell* in the tree when it came down.'

'Oh—exactly.'

'Certainly. I unwound the lariat, and fastened one end of

it to the limb. It was the best green rawhide, and capable of sustaining tons. I made a slip noose in the other end, and then hung it down to see the length. It reached down twenty-two feet—halfway to the ground. I then loaded every barrel of the Allen with a double charge. I felt satisfied. I said to myself, if he never thinks of that one thing that I dread, all right—but if he does, all right anyhow—I am fixed for him. But don't you know that the very thing a man dreads is the thing that always happens? Indeed it is so. I watched the bull, now, with anxiety—anxiety which no one can conceive of who has not been in such a situation and felt that at any moment death might come. Presently a thought came into the bull's eye. I knew it said I—if my nerve fails now, I am lost. Sure enough, it was just as I had dreaded, he started in to climb the tree—'

'What, the bull?'

'Of course—who else?'

'But a bull can't climb a tree.'

'He can't, can't he? Since you know so much about it, did you ever see a bull try?'

'No! I never dreamt of such a thing.'

'Well, then, what is the use of your talking that way, then? Because you never saw a thing done, is that any reason why it can't be done?'

'Well, all right—go on. What did you do?'

'The bull started up, and got along well for about ten feet, then slipped and slid back. I breathed easier. He tried it again—got up a little higher—slipped again. But he came at it once more, and this time he was careful. He got gradually higher and higher, and my spirits went down more and more. Up he came—an inch at a time—with his eyes hot, and his tongue hanging out. Higher and higher—hitched his foot over the stump of a limb, and looked up, as much as to say, "You are my meat, friend." Up again—higher and higher, and getting more excited the closer he got. He was within ten feet of me!

37

I took a long breath—and then said I, "It is now or
never." I had the coil of the lariat all ready; I paid it out
slowly, till it hung right over his head; all of a sudden
I let go of the slack, and the slip noose fell fairly round
his neck! Quicker than lightning I out with the Allen
and let him have it in the face. It was an awful roar,
and must have scared the bull out of his senses. When
the smoke cleared away, there he was, dangling in the
air, twenty foot from the ground, and going out of one
convulsion into another faster than you could count!
I didn't stop to count, anyhow—I shinned down the tree
and shot for home.'

'Bemis, is all that true, just as you have stated it?'

'I wish I may rot in my tracks and die the death of a
dog if it isn't.'

'Well, we can't refuse to believe it, and we don't. But if
there were some proofs—'

'Proofs? Did I bring back my lariat?'

'No.'

'Did I bring back my horse?'

'No.'

'Did you ever see the bull again?'

'No.'

'Well, then, what more do you want? I never saw anybody as particular as you are about a thing like that.'

I made up my mind that if this man was not a liar he
only missed it by the skin of his teeth.

Roughing It, vol. 1, ch. 7

Bemis's tale is, of course, a burlesque of the 'noble
sport' of buffalo hunting. From the time when the buffalo
turns on Bemis the story moves through a series of increasingly ridiculous possibilities, culminating in the bull hanging itself while pursuing Bemis up a tree. The events
described in Bemis's dead-pan voice are so incredible, that
it becomes evident that his intention in telling the story is

not to deceive his audience. His adventures are too incredible ever to be believed at a literal level; lies must sound like the truth if they are to succeed. Also, the questions his audience put to him seem less designed to catch him out, than to provoke him into even wilder exaggerations and more absurd arguments. Bemis's story is not rejected by the audience, but is accepted for what it is, a comic experience in which they all take part. On a psychological level Bemis's tall tale may be a substitute for anger, and a means by which he counteracts his humiliation. Instead of accepting his disgrace, he creates a fantasy out of his experience, with himself as hero. There is a strong element of ritual in the tall story that the question and answer structure makes evident. By his humiliating accident Bemis cut himself away from the rest of the company, and his tall tale is a method of re-establishing his relationship through a ritualistic tale-telling in which all take part.

Anticlimax

A typical and recurrent situation in Mark Twain's humour is one where the expectations of a scene or character are suddenly reversed, and the values inherent in the original situation are mocked and destroyed. In the next extract, Tom Sawyer acts out the role of the Sunday school 'good' boy; in order to impress his new beloved Becky Thatcher, he poses as one who has learned two thousand verses of the Bible! He is then called on to display his wisdom before Judge Thatcher and the assembled Sunday school.

12

Tom was introduced to the Judge; but his tongue was tied, his breath would hardly come, his heart quaked—

partly because of the awful greatness of the man, but mainly because he was *her* parent. He would have liked to fall down and worship him, if it were in the dark. The Judge put his hand on Tom's head and called him a fine little man, and asked him what his name was. The boy stammered, gasped, and got it out:

'Tom.'

'Oh, no, not Tom—it is—'

'Thomas.'

'Ah, that's it. I thought there was more to it, maybe. That's very well. But you've another one I daresay, and you'll tell it to me, won't you?'

'Tell the gentleman your other name, Thomas,' said Walters, 'and say *sir*. You mustn't forget your manners.'

'Thomas Sawyer—sir.'

'That's it! That's a good boy. Fine boy. Fine, manly little fellow. Two thousand verses is a great many—very, very great many. And you never can be sorry for the trouble you took to learn them; for knowledge is worth more than anything there is in the world; it's what makes great men and good men; you'll be a great man and a good man yourself, some day, Thomas, and then you'll look back and say, It's all owing to the precious Sunday-school privileges of my boyhood—it's all owing to my dear teachers that taught me to learn—it's all owing to the good superintendent, who encouraged me, and watched over me, and gave me a beautiful Bible—a splendid elegant Bible—to keep and have it all for my own, always—it's all owing to right bringing up! That is what you will say, Thomas—and you wouldn't take any money for those two thousand verses—no indeed you wouldn't. And now you wouldn't mind telling me and this lady some of the things you've learned—no, I know you wouldn't—for we are proud of little boys that learn. Now, no doubt you know the names of all the twelve disciples. Won't you tell us the names of the first two that were appointed?'

Tom was tugging at a buttonhole and looking sheepish. He blushed, now, and his eyes fell. Mr. Walters' heart sank within him. He said to himself, it is not possible that the boy can answer the simplest question—why *did* the Judge ask him? Yet he felt obliged to speak up and say:

'Answer the gentleman, Thomas—don't be afraid.'

Tom still hung fire.

'Now I know you'll tell *me*,' said the lady. 'The names of the first two disciples were—'

'DAVID AND GOLIATH!'

Let us draw the curtain of charity over the rest of the scene.

The Adventures of Tom Sawyer, ch. 4

The chapter from which this extract is taken is entitled 'Showing Off in Sunday School', and earlier Twain had described the showing off antics of Tom and his teacher Mr. Walters. Now responsible adult behaviour is linked with childhood, and we see Judge Thatcher himself furiously showing off before the Sunday school audience. What is being gently mocked here is not Tom or his ignorance, but Judge Thatcher whose pompous and patronizing behaviour is reduced to farce when Tom's long-awaited answer turns out to be utter nonsense. The Judge's speech is made up from outworn clichés—'precious Sunday-school privileges', 'splendid elegant Bible'—and so is his system of moral values which he dwells on so lovingly because he is sure he embodies it. The unspoken implication is that Tom could grow up to be great and good like Judge Thatcher—and a pompous ass! Further irony is added to this scene if we recall Tom Sawyer's function in *Huckleberry Finn*: there he is a junior Judge Thatcher, continually showing off, and upholding conventional standards of thought and feeling.

The final extract in this chapter also involves the use of

anticlimax. The new judge in *Huckleberry Finn* makes a parade of his charity and piety by attempting to reform Pap Finn, the village drunkard.

13

When he got out the new judge said he was a-going to make a man of him. So he took him to his own house, and dressed him up clean and nice, and had him to breakfast and dinner and supper with the family, and was just old pie to him, so to speak. And after supper he talked to him about temperance and such things till the old man cried, and said he'd been a fool, and fooled away his life; but now he was a-going to turn over a new leaf and be a man nobody wouldn't be ashamed of, and he hoped the judge would help him and not look down on him. The judge said he could hug him for them words; so *he* cried and his wife she cried again; pap said he'd been a man that had always been misunderstood before, and the judge said he believed it. The old man said that what a man wanted that was down was sympathy, and the judge said it was so; so they cried again. And when it was bedtime the old man rose up and held out his hand, and says:

'Look at it, gentlemen and ladies all; take a-hold of it; shake it. There's a hand that was the hand of a hog; but it ain't so no more; it's the hand of a man that's started in on a new life, and'll die before he'll go back. You mark them words—don't forget I said them. It's a clean hand now; shake it—don't be afeard.'

So they shook it, one after the other, all around, and cried. The judge's wife she kissed it. Then the old man he signed a pledge—made his mark. The judge said it was the holiest time on record, or something like that. Then they tucked the old man into a beautiful room, which was the spare room, and in the night some time he got powerful thirsty and clumb out on to the porch-roof and slid down a stanchion and traded his new coat for a jug of forty-rod, and clumb back again and had a good old time; and toward daylight he crawled out again, drunk as a fiddler, and rolled off the porch and broke his left arm in two places, and was most froze to death when somebody found him after sun-up. And when they come to look at that spare room they had to take soundings before they could navigate it.

The judge he felt kind of sore. He said he reckoned a body could reform the old man with a shotgun, maybe, but he didn't know no other way.

Huckleberry Finn, ch. 5

What is being mocked here is not Pap Finn's degeneration, but the notions of easy and instant moral reform which the judge attempts to put into practice in his one-man campaign. The judge's belief in the possibility of a 'new life' is naïve, sentimental, and transitory. He is interested in Pap Finn not as a person, but as a figure in a self-indulgent charade, and his basic insincerity is mirrored in his silly behaviour; his gestures and responses are all overdone, as if he were taking part in a temperance melodrama. For a time Pap Finn plays his role successfully; he even takes over the centre of the stage and mimics the judge's temperance rhetoric. But Pap can't sustain his role; he literally falls back into reality, only to be abandoned by his benefactor. The last words ironically reveal the limits of the judge's gaudy Christian tolerance and charity.

Character portrayal

In July, 1885 Clemens wrote to William Dean Howells describing the difficulties he had encountered in reading *Middlemarch*; for him the experience had been totally unrewarding and tedious:

I can't stand George Eliot and Hawthorne and those people; I see what they are at a hundred years before they get to it and they just tire me to death. And as for 'The Bostonians', I would rather be damned to John Bunyan's heaven than read that.

Clemens's remarks in this letter are characteristic of his attitude to fiction, and they point to a paradox in his work: he was a successful novelist, yet he had little interest in the novel either as a tradition or as a literary form. Mark Twain was fundamentally a humorist, and his comic imagination was more successful in the creation of character than of plot. In his travel books Clemens created not a new form but a new character called 'Mark Twain' with a fresh perspective and outlook on the world, while in the novels the imperfect structures are less important than the wonderful characters who inhabit them.

Mark Twain's first novel, *The Gilded Age*, is a fragmentary and confused book that unsuccessfully combines Warner's sentimental melodrama with Twain's satire on the feverish speculation, the social and political corruption, and the overall vulgarity of General Grant's administration. The complicated and dull narrative design of the novel is offset by Twain's invention of Colonel Eschol Sellers, a character who plays little part in the plot of the novel, but who dominates its life. He is the figure who represents the fatal uncritical optimism of the era to which the novel has given a name; a dreamer who ignores the sordid reality at his feet, and who fixes his mind on an imaginary world of his own possibilities. In the following extract one of the heroes of the novel, young Washington Hawkins, has arrived in the town of Hawkeye, Missouri, to seek fame and fortune with the help of the visionary Colonel Sellers. He pays an unexpected visit on the Colonel and is invited to sit down to dinner with the family.

14

'All right, my boy, all right—always glad to see you— always glad to hear your voice and take you by the hand. Don't wait for special invitations—that's all nonsense among friends. Just come whenever you can, and come as often as you can—the oftener the better. You can't please us any better than that, Washington; the little woman will tell you so herself. We don't pretend to style. Plain folks, you know—plain folks. Just a plain family dinner, but such as it is, our friends are *always* welcome, I reckon you know that yourself, Washington. Run along, children, run along; Lafayette,* stand off the

* In those old days the average man called his children after his most revered literary and historical idols; consequently there was hardly a family, at least in the West, but had a Washington in it—and also a Lafayette, a Franklin, and six or eight

cat's tail, child, can't you see what you're doing?

'Come, come, come, Roderick Dhu, it isn't nice for little boys to hang on to young gentlemen's coat tails— but never mind him, Washington, he's full of spirits, and don't mean any harm. Children will be children, you know. Take the chair next to Mrs. Sellers, Washington —tut, tut, Marie Antoinette, let your brother have the fork if he wants it, you are bigger than he is.'

Washington contemplated the banquet, and wondered if he were in his right mind. Was this the plain family dinner? And was it all present? It was soon apparent that this was indeed the dinner: it was all on the table: it consisted of abundance of clear, fresh water, and a basin of raw turnips—nothing more.

Washington stole a glance at Mrs. Sellers' face, and would have given the world, the next moment, if he could have spared her that. The poor woman's face was crimson, and the tears stood in her eyes. Washington did not know what to do. He wished he had never come there and spied out this cruel poverty, and brought pain to that poor little lady's heart and shame to her cheek; but he was there, and there was no escape. Colonel Sellers hitched back his coat-sleeves airily from his wrists as who should say, 'Now for solid enjoyment!' seized a fork, flourished it, and began to harpoon turnips and deposit them in the plates before him:

'Let me help you, Washington—Lafayette, pass this plate to Washington—ah, well, well, my boy, things are looking pretty bright now, I tell you. Speculation—my! the whole atmosphere's full of money. I wouldn't take three fortunes for one little operation I've got on hand now—have anything from the casters? No? Well, you're

sounding names from Byron, Scott, and the Bible, if the offspring held out. To visit such a family, was to find oneself confronted by a congress made up of representatives of the imperial myths and the majestic dead of all the ages. There was something thrilling about it, to a stranger, not to say awe-inspiring.

right, you're right. Some people like mustard with turnips, but—now there was Baron Poniatowski—Lord, but that man did know how to live!—true Russian, you know, Russian to the backbone; I say to my wife, give me a Russian every time for a table comrade. The Baron used to say, "Take mustard, Sellers, try the mustard,—a man *can't* know what turnips are in perfection without mustard," but I always said, "No, Baron, I'm a plain man, and I want my food plain—none of your embellishments for Eschol Sellers—no made dishes for me!" And it's the best way—high living kills more than it cures in this world, you can rest assured of that. Yes, indeed, Washington, I've got one little operation on hand that—take some more water—help yourself, won't you?—help yourself, there's plenty of it. You'll find it pretty good, I guess. How does that fruit strike you?'

Washington said he did not know that he had ever tasted better. He did not add that he detested turnips even when they were cooked—loathed them in their natural state. No, he kept this to himself, and praised the turnips to the peril of his soul.

'I thought you'd like them. Examine them—examine them—they'll bear it. See how perfectly firm and juicy they are—they can't start any like them in this part of the country, I can tell you. These are from New Jersey—I imported them myself. They cost like sin, too; but, Lord bless me, I go in for having the best of a thing, even if it does cost a little more—it's the best economy in the long run. These are the Early Malcolm—it's a turnip that can't be produced except in just one orchard, and the supply never is up to the demand. Take some more water, Washington—you can't drink too much water with fruit— all the doctors say that. The plague can't come where this article is, my boy!'

The Gilded Age, ch. 11

The comedy in this situation derives from the incongruity between the reality of poverty, and the fantastic world of illusions which the Colonel's imagination creates. When Washington sees the 'banquet' before him he sees it in the matter of fact light of reality as a basin of raw turnips. But Colonel Sellers, despite his description of himself as a 'plain man' possesses a transforming imagination which removes everything out of the realm of the commonplace. The mention of mustard leads him into a monologue on a totally imaginary Russian nobleman, while the solidly enjoyed turnips are transformed into 'fruit' and given a pedigree. Necessity and poverty are transformed by the Colonel's humour not only into pleasure—(turnips become 'fruit') but into benefits—these wonderful 'fruit' save the eater from being infected by the plague! The Colonel here is engaged in one of the basic functions of humour—the transformation through the imagination of a dull or unpleasant reality into enjoyable fantasy. Notice that Washington has little opportunity to dwell on the poverty of Colonel Sellers and his family, because he is so enthralled by the Colonel's monologue. The Colonel's outstanding characteristic is his grandiose imagination, similar in some respects to that of the King and the Duke in *Huckleberry Finn*, except that, despite his lines, the Colonel never intends to deceive. The King and the Duke invent personal fantasies in order to gull and defraud ignorant people, but the Colonel's fantasies are his reality, and his ultimate purpose is to create pleasure and wonder. But Colonel Sellers can hardly be considered a fully rounded fictional character. Clemens's technique involves the exaggeration of the Colonel's imagination to the exclusion of any other characteristics; what we encounter here is more of a caricature than a personality.

Few of the characters in Clemens's novels are described

in their external appearances. We learn little of what Colonel Sellers looks like, or Tom Sawyer, Huckleberry Finn, Pudd'nhead Wilson, and Hank Morgan. We learn about these characters through their talk rather than through their appearances; they reveal themselves to us in their speech. A partial exception is Pap Finn; when Huck first encounters him he describes him in the following way :

15

He was most fifty, and he looked it. His hair was long and tangled and greasy, and hung down, and you could see his eyes shining through like he was behind vines. It was all black, no gray; so was his long, mixed-up whiskers. There warn't no color in his face, where his face showed; it was white; not like another man's white, but a white to make a body sick, a white to make a body's flesh crawl— a tree-toad white, a fish-belly white. As for his clothes— just rags, that was all. He had one ankle resting on t'other knee; the boot on that foot was busted, and two of his toes stuck through, and he worked them now and then. His hat was laying on the floor—an old black slouch with the top caved in, like a lid.

Huckleberry Finn, ch. 5

We have already encountered Pap Finn in the previous chapter, when his drunken spree forms a comic anti-climax to the judge's pious attempts to reform him. But here he is far from being a comic figure. The description is not generalized; certain features of Pap's appearance are picked out and emphasized. He is described in terms of black and white, both colours associated with death, and his appearance is at the same time sinister and

49

repulsive. The details build up a picture of degeneration—his hair, face, colour, boots, and hat, and Huck's likening his absence of facial colour to a tree-toad, and a fish's belly, suggest not only physical loathsomeness, but also death—a dead fish always floats belly upwards. This physical description of Pap prepares us not only for his death (he dies on the river), but for the moral role he plays in the book. He sleeps with the pigs in the town tanyard, and his attitudes and behaviour are akin to his physical appearance. He captures Huck and locks him in a hut on the river banks. There he abuses him, beats him and almost murders him; he also treats him to the following lecture on 'govment':

16

'Oh, yes, this is a wonderful govment, wonderful. Why, looky here. There was a free nigger there from Ohio—a mulatter, most as white as a white man. He had the whitest shirt on you ever see, too, and the shiniest hat; and there ain't a man in that town that's got as fine clothes as what he had; and he had a gold watch and chain, and a silver-headed cane—the awfulest old gray-headed nabob in the state. And what do you think? They said he was a p'fessor in a college, and could talk all kinds of languages, and knowed everything. And that ain't the wust. They said he could *vote* when he was at home. Well, that let me out. Thinks I, what is the country a-coming to? It was 'lection day, and I was just about to go and vote myself if I warn't too drunk to get there; but when they told me there was a state in this country where they'd let that nigger vote, I drawed out. I says I'll never vote ag'in. Them's the very words I said; they all heard me; and the country may rot for all me—I'll never vote ag'in as long as I live. And to see the cool way of that nigger—why, he wouldn't 'a' give me the road if I hadn't shoved him out o' the way. I says to the people, why ain't this nigger put up at auction and sold —that's what I want to know. And what do you reckon they said? Why, they said he couldn't be sold till he'd been in the state six months, and he hadn't been there that long yet. There, now—that's a specimen. They call that a govment that can't sell a free nigger till he's been in the state six months. Here's a govment that calls itself a govment, and lets on to be a govment, and thinks it is a govment, and yet's got to set stock-still for six whole months before it can take a-hold of a prowling, thieving, infernal, white-shirted free nigger, and—'

Pap was a-going on so he never noticed where his old limber legs was taking him to, so he went head over heels over the tub of salt pork and barked both shins, and the rest of his speech was all the hottest kind of language— mostly hove at the nigger and the govment, though he gave the tub some, too, all along, here and there. He hopped around the cabin considerable, first on one leg and then on the other, holding first one shin and then the other one, and at last he let out with his left foot all of a sudden and fetched the tub a rattling kick. But it warn't good judgment, because that was the boot that had a couple of his toes leaking out of the front end of it; so now he raised a howl that fairly made a body's hair raise, and down he went in the dirt, and rolled there, and held his toes; and the cussing he done then laid over anything he had ever done previous. He said so his own self afterwards. He had heard old Sowberry Hagan in his best days, and he said it laid over him, too; but I reckon that was sort of piling it on, maybe.

Huckleberry Finn, ch. 6

Pap Finn comes from the lowest depths of white society; he is a tramp, a thief, and a drunkard, but he still fiercely and jealously guards his status as a white man. His monologue, provoked by the sight of a well-dressed free Negro, could be the outburst of an ignorant racialist, were it not for the fact that his views are merely an extension of the attitudes held by decent, pious folk like Miss Watson, homely families like the Phelpses, and even well-brought-up children like Tom Sawyer. The effectiveness of Pap's speech is that it puts into language the assumptions of his social betters, and at least Pap's reasons for jealousy are clear and understandable—he envies the Negro's dress, his hat, etc., and he feels himself to be a man without 'rights', since he wears a two piece hat, and exists as an outcast. His outburst is at least understandable, and derives from a need to feel important as a human being—but how can we defend the actions of Miss Watson, the Phelpses, or the 'aristocratic' King and Duke towards Jim?

Perhaps it is not very accurate to see Pap's outburst in terms of racial prejudice. It is not Negroes he rages at but *a Negro*, and he has no theories to promote of racial superiority. In fact, the villain in Pap's melodrama is not the Negro but the 'govment' on which he takes revenge with words; his technique is to turn reality upside down and play at possessing a status he does not have. Despite his outburst Pap is not altogether an obnoxious character; there is surely a kind of grandeur in his outburst. And even when his diatribe is deflated by his falling over a barrel, he still retains some dignity. Even if he can't achieve personal or social success he can still be a success-ful swearer! Immediately afterwards Pap ceases to be a comic figure; his degenerate grandeur vanishes and he takes refuge in a drunken spree that, unlike the previous episode, has no trace of humour. Here Pap is a suffering figure in his own right, and he is no longer used to parody bourgeois notions of moral reform.

17

I don't know how long I was asleep, but all of a sudden there was an awful scream and I was up. There was pap, looking wild and skipping around every which way and yelling about snakes. He said they was crawling up his legs; and then he would give a jump and scream, and say one had bit him on the cheek—but I couldn't see no snakes. He started and run round and round the cabin, hollering 'take him off! take him off! he's biting me on the neck!' I never see a man look so wild in the eyes. Pretty soon he was all fagged out, and fell down panting; then he rolled over and over, wonderful fast, kicking things every which way, and striking and grabbing at the air with his hands, and screaming, and saying there was devils ahold of him. He wore out, by-and-by, and laid still a while, moaning. Then he laid stiller, and didn't make a sound. I could hear the owls and the wolves, away off in the woods, and it seemed terrible still. He was laying over by the corner. By-and-by he raised up, part way, and listened, with his head to one side. He says very low:

'Tramp—tramp—tramp; that's the dead; tramp—tramp —tramp; they're coming after me; but I won't go. Oh, they're here! don't touch me—don't! hands off—they're cold; let go. Oh, let a poor devil alone!'

Then he went down on all fours and crawled off, begging them to let him alone, and he rolled himself up in his blanket and wallowed in under the old pine table, still a-begging; and then he went crying. I could hear him through the blanket.

By and by he rolled out and jumped up to his feet looking wild, and he see me and went for me. He chased me round and round the place with a clasp-knife, calling me the Angel of Death, and saying he would kill me, and then I couldn't come for him no more. I begged, and told him I was only Huck; but he laughed *such* a

53

screechy laugh, and roared and cussed, and kept on chasing me up. Once when I turned short and dodged under his arm he made a grab and got me by the jacket between my shoulders, and I thought I was gone; but I slid out of the jacket quick as lightning, and saved myself. Pretty soon he was all tired out, and dropped down with his back against the door, and said he would rest a minute and then kill me. He put his knife under him, and said he would sleep and get strong, and then he would see who was who.

Huckleberry Finn, ch. 6

From being a comic figure Pap Finn changes until we see him here a figure of pity and terror. The premonitions of death in the original description of Pap are brought to a climax here in the nightmare visitors—snakes, devils, and the tramping dead, culminating in Huck as the Angel of Death. Huck's sense of death in Ch. 1 is repeated here; the stillness is broken by the cries of wolves and owls, both harbingers of death. The claustrophobic terror is reinforced by the locked cabin, and the scene is skilfully narrated by Twain switching from Pap's terror-stricken outburst to Huck's sensitive observations. And Huck is never simply a narrator standing back and looking. He too is deeply involved; the terror of death is close to his unconsciousness too, and the man cowering in agony under the table is his father.

Huck's encounter with violence and terror in the confines of the closed cabin are perhaps a prefiguration of what he will encounter in the rest of the book. His relationship with his father moves from farce to terror, but so do many of Huck's experiences. Huck's relationship with his father also provokes another critical question. Both are outcasts, one is father, the other son, and both live in a similar environment of violence, hypocrisy and corruption; both are haunted by thoughts of death. Could it be that Pap is an older version of Huck, and is Pap's fate the penalty of non-conformity?

The most complex and fully developed character in Mark Twain's fiction is Huckleberry Finn, and while there is no opportunity here for a full examination of the character, the next extract illustrates the way he comes to a decision in an important crisis. The journey on the raft has taken Jim far down river away from the planned escape route to the North, and the King has sold him to Silas Phelps as a runaway slave for $40. The search for freedom is finished, as Huck says, 'all come to nothing, everything all busted up and ruined', and he has now to face up to the problem he had evaded before—whether to tell Miss Watson of Jim's whereabouts.

18

Once I said to myself it would be a thousand times better for Jim to be a slave at home where his family was, as long as he'd *got* to be a slave, and so I'd better write a letter to Tom Sawyer and tell him to tell Miss Watson where he was. But I soon give up that notion for two things; she'd be mad and disgusted at his rascality and ungratefulness for leaving her, and so she'd sell him straight down the river again; and if she didn't, everybody naturally despises an ungrateful nigger, and they'd make Jim feel it all the time, and so he'd feel ornery and disgraced. And then think of *me!* It would get all around that Huck Finn helped a nigger to get his freedom; and if I was ever to see anybody from that town again I'd be ready to get down and lick his boots for shame. That's just the way: a person does a low-down thing, and then he don't want to take no consequences of it. Thinks as long as he can hide, it ain't no disgrace. That was my fix exactly. The more I studied about this the more my conscience went to grinding me, and the more wicked and low-down and ornery I got to feeling. And at last, when it hit me all of a sudden that here was the plain hand of Providence slapping me in the face and letting me know my wickedness was being watched all the time from up there in heaven, whilst I was stealing a poor old woman's nigger that hadn't ever done me no harm, and now was showing me there's One that's always on the lookout, and ain't a-going to allow no such miserable doings to go only just so fur and no further, I most dropped in my tracks I was so scared. Well, I tried the best I could to kinder soften it up somehow for myself by saying I was brung up wicked, and so I warn't so much to blame; but something inside of me kept saying, 'There was the Sunday-school, you could 'a' gone to it; and if you'd 'a' done it they'd 'a' learnt you there that people that acts as I'd been acting about that nigger goes to everlasting fire.'

It made me shiver. And I about made up my mind to pray, and see if I couldn't try to quit being the kind of a boy I was and be better. So I kneeled down. But the words wouldn't come. Why wouldn't they? It warn't no use to try and hide it from Him. Nor from *me*, neither. I knowed very well why they wouldn't come. It was because my heart warn't right; it was because I warn't square; it was because I was playing double. I was letting *on* to give up sin, but away inside of me I was holding on to the biggest one of all. I was trying to make my mouth *say* I would do the right thing and the clean thing, and go and write to that nigger's owner and tell where he was; but deep down in me I knowed it was a lie, and He knowed it. You can't pray a lie—I found that out.

So I was full of trouble, full as I could be; and didn't know what to do. At last I had an idea; and I says, I'll go and write the letter—and *then* see if I can pray. Why, it was astonishing, the way I felt as light as a feather, right straight off, and my troubles all gone. So I got a piece of paper and a pencil, all glad and excited, and set down and wrote:

Miss Watson your runaway nigger Jim is down here two mile below Pikesville and Mr Phelps has got him and he will give him up for the reward if you send.

HUCK FINN

I felt good and all washed clean of sin for the first time I had ever felt so in my life, and I knowed I could pray now. But I didn't do it straight off, but laid the paper down and set there thinking—thinking how good it was all this happened so, and how near I come to being lost and going to hell. And went on thinking. And got to thinking over our trip down the river; and I see Jim before me, all the time, in the day, and in the night-time, sometimes moonlight, sometimes storms, and we a floating along, talking, and singing, and laughing. But somehow I couldn't seem to strike no places to harden me against him, but only the other kind. I'd see him standing my watch on top of his'n, stead of calling me, so I could go on sleeping; and see him how glad he was when I come back out of the fog; and when I come to him again in the swamp, up there where the feud was; and such-like times; and would always call me honey, and pet me, and do everything he could think of for me, and how good he always was; and at last I struck the time I saved him by telling the men we had small-pox aboard, and he was so grateful, and said I was the best friend old Jim ever had in the world, and the *only* one he's got now; and then I happened to look around, and see that paper.

It was a close place. I took it up, and held it in my hand. I was a trembling, because I'd got to decide, forever, betwixt two things, and I knowed it. I studied a minute, sort of holding my breath, and then says to myself:

'All right, then, I'll *go* to hell'—and tore it up.
Huckleberry Finn, ch. 31

This passage brings to a crisis a central conflict between Huck's loyalty to standards and values he knows and believes to be right. The fact that we do not believe in Huck's social values does not invalidate their importance for him; even at the height of his moral crisis he does not believe that he is being anything but wicked, and he has no doubts about the institution of slavery. Huck's debate follows two paths. First, he decides to write to Miss Watson, then he does so—but he can't live with his decision, so he tears up the letter and accepts the consequences. At the beginning of the passage Huck finds altruistic reasons for writing to Miss Watson—Jim would be better off at home! But Huck's real concern is about his own status not Jim's; he soon gives up the letter-writing idea because it would become known that *he* had helped Jim to freedom. His feelings for Jim at this stage are stifled by self-interest and fear of public opinion; he is thwarted by the memory of 'good' people, by values outside himself.

The next stage in Huck's debate with himself comes when he is faced with a more formidable social and moral arbiter—his own conscience. Huck's conscience is not a free agent, it is the product of his environment. Eventually the 'grinding' conscience takes over Huck's mind; he begins to think along the lines his conscience dictates. This is mirrored in the sentimental rhetoric ('poor old woman'), the rag ends of naïve religion ('plain hand of Providence', 'hide it from Him', 'my heart war'nt right', 'the clean thing'). The language here is unlike Huck's usual vivid vernacular, it is awkward and stilted, as if he were remembering scraps of Sunday school jargon. He is preoccupied with sin, cleanness, and fear of Hell and damnation. He finally submits to his conscience—the King's 'hogwash' which we see in operation at the revival meeting. He writes the letter to Miss Watson and immediately experiences a psychic benefit: 'I felt good and all washed clean of sin'—these are not Huck's own words, but those of the moral revivalists.

But Huck's next thought reverses his decision. His conscience having extracted its token sacrifice subsides, and in the ensuing peace a lower level of Huck's consciousness comes to life, more real and more elemental feelings overcome him in his memory of Jim. So the language changes —the stilted forms, the language of gentility, refinement, and morality give way to the unique vernacular of Huck; a language of sensation and feeling rather than of ideology. Huck's memory of Jim begins in gladness ('singing and laughing'), and ends in love. His decision to tear up the letter has not come from understanding, but from feeling, an unspoken recognition that he will sacrifice duty, honour, respectability, even Heaven for the sake of their love. This passage draws together two important aspects of *Huckleberry Finn*—the theme of freedom and of social satire; they are filtered through the unique consciousness of Huck Finn and told in his unique way.

Style and description

The central theme of the 'Old Times' section of *Life on the Mississippi* concerns the education of Mark Twain, the young cub pilot, and his initiation into the mysteries of navigating the great river. This education involves more than the arduous learning of the shifting and ambiguous physical character of the river; it is also a moral education that requires the young boy to develop within himself mature qualities of courage and self-reliance. It is this knowledge of the river that distinguishes the viewpoints of the initiated pilot and the inexperienced passengers; when the passengers look at the river they see 'pretty pictures', but to the eye of the pilot it takes on the form of the 'grimmest and most dead-earnest' reality. Yet, Mark Twain also suggests that the naïve viewpoint of the passengers possesses a quality which the pilot's realism lacks; the quality of romance. In learning the true nature of the river the pilot loses the ability to enjoy its beauty in a superficial romantic manner, as the following description of sunset on the Mississippi illustrates.

19

Now when I had mastered the language of this water and had come to know every trifling feature that bordered the great river as familiarly as I knew the letters of the alphabet, I had made a valuable acquisition. But I had lost something, too. I had lost something which could never be restored to me while I lived. All the grace, the beauty, the poetry had gone out of the majestic river! I still keep in mind a certain wonderful sunset which I witnessed when steamboating was new to me. A broad expanse of the river was turned to blood; in the middle distance the red hue brightened into gold, through which a solitary log came floating, black and conspicuous; in one place a long, slanting mark lay sparkling upon the water; in another the surface was broken by boiling, tumbling rings, that were as many-tinted as an opal; where the ruddy flush was faintest, was a smooth spot that was covered with graceful circles and radiating lines, ever so delicately traced; the shore on our left was densely wooded, and the sombre shadow that fell from this forest was broken in one place by a long, ruffled trail that shone like silver; and high above the forest wall a clean-stemmed dead tree waved a single leafy bough that glowed like a flame in the unobstructed splendor that was flowing from the sun. There were graceful curves, reflected images, woody heights, soft distances; and over the whole scene, far and near, the dissolving lights drifted steadily, enriching it, every passing moment, with new marvels of coloring.

I stood like one bewitched. I drank it in, in a speechless rapture. The world was new to me, and I had never seen anything like this at home. But as I have said, a day came when I began to cease from noting the glories and the charms which the moon and the sun and the twilight wrought upon the river's face; another day came when I ceased altogether to note them. Then, if that sunset scene had been repeated, I should have looked upon it without rapture, and should have commented upon it, inwardly, after this fashion: This sun means that we are going to have wind tomorrow; that floating log means that the river is rising, small thanks to it; that slanting mark on the water refers to a bluff reef which is going to kill somebody's steamboat one of these nights, if it keeps on stretching out like that; those tumbling 'boils' show a dissolving bar and a changing channel there; the lines and circles in the slick water over yonder are a warning that that troublesome place is shoaling up dangerously; that silver streak in the shadow of the forest is the 'break' from a new snag, and he has located himself in the very best place he could have found to fish for steamboats; that tall dead tree, with a single living branch, is not going to last long, and then how is a body ever going to get through this blind place at night without the friendly old landmark?

No, the romance and the beauty were all gone from the river. All the value any feature of it had for me now was the amount of usefulness it could furnish toward compassing the safe piloting of a steamboat. Since those days, I have pitied doctors from my heart. What does the lovely flush in a beauty's cheek mean to a doctor but a 'break' that ripples above some deadly disease? Are not all her visible charms sown thick with what are to him the signs and symbols of hidden decay? Does he ever see her beauty at all, or doesn't he simply view her professionally, and comment upon her unwholesome condition all to himself? And doesn't he sometimes wonder whether he has gained most or lost most by learning his trade?

Life on the Mississippi, ch. 9

This passage describes two radically different ways of experiencing the same landscape, the romantic and the realistic, and at first sight Clemens may appear to be coming down firmly on the side of the romantic viewpoint, since he laments the loss of 'the grace, the beauty, the poetry' that realism necessitates. But if we examine the passage more carefully we discover that the romantic description is stylized, conventional, and cliché-ridden. All individual apprehension is lost in the vague and pretentious descriptive language, which derives from a tradition of writing equivalent to sentimental landscape painting. Terms like 'graceful circles', 'radiating lines', 'graceful curves', 'soft distances' and 'dissolving lights' are all clichés of art criticism, but do they give any real sense of how the landscape looked or how the observer felt? The observer's feelings when he looks at the sunset are described in vague and generalized terms—'I stood like one bewitched', 'speechless rapture', and his likening of the boiling many-hued river to an opal is surely rather a banal anticlimax. Clemens is working here firmly within the framework of conventional rhetoric. The passage reads like the description of a second rate Victorian landscape painting; there is a rather obvious use of contrasting colours, while the melodramatic dead tree with its 'single leafy bough' is a picturesque device from romantic painting. It is the kind of landscape one could imagine being the focus of admiration in the Grangerford home, along with the chromos and plaster fruit. The last paragraph is equally awkward and artificial. The elaborate rhetorical question about the doctor and the 'lovely flush' on the beauty's cheek adds nothing to what has gone before, and is remarkable only for its banality. The overall tone of the passage is derived from the hackneyed conventions of landscape art, apart from the last paragraph which seems inspired by the sentimental fiction of the day—the fiction that Clemens despised as 'slush'.

The description of the sunset on the Mississippi is vague, conventional, and derivative; it is also typical of the stylistic confusion created by Twain when he attempted the role of the genteel man of letters. The following description of a view from Virginia City illustrates the absurdities of popular sentimentalism.

20

From Virginia's airy situation one could look over a vast, far-reaching panorama, of mountain ranges and deserts; and whether the day was bright or overcast, whether the sun was rising or setting, or flaming in the zenith, or whether night and the moon held sway, the spectacle was always impressive and beautiful. Over your head Mount Davidson lifted its gray dome, and before and below you a rugged canyon clove the battlemented hills, making a somber gateway through which a soft-tinted desert was glimpsed, with the silver thread of a river winding through it, bordered with trees which many miles of distance diminished to a delicate fringe; and still further away the snowy mountains rose up and stretched their long barrier to the filmy horizon—far enough beyond a lake that burned in the desert like a fallen sun, though that, itself, lay fifty miles removed. Look from your window where you would, there was fascination in the picture. At rare intervals—but very rare—there were clouds in our skies, and then the setting sun would gild and flush and glorify this mighty expanse of scenery with a bewildering pomp of color that held the eye like a spell and moved the spirit like music.

Roughing It, vol. 11, ch. 2

There is no sense here of an individually apprehended landscape, instead the scene is a 'picture' which Twain observes through a pseudo-cultural 'Claude-glass'. From his 'airy situation' he sees a 'spectacle' of 'battlemented hills' and 'soft-tinted desert' extending to a 'filmy horizon'. We can't believe in the scene because Twain can't describe it adequately; the prose is dead and artificial, ('gild and flush and glorify'), and there is no sense that Twain is being deliberately ironic in order to mock the clichés of

64

conventional description. As a pilot on the river, Twain came to grief when he indulged in self-deception and romantic posturing, and what applied to the art of piloting also held good for the craft of writing. In order to become a good pilot he had to be courageous and self-reliant (see extract 5), and in order to become a good writer he had to avoid this kind of formal pretentiousness. Yet the alternative which Twain puts forward in *Life on the Mississippi* to the sentimental extravaganza, is hardly more satisfactory—a dull, objective, pragmatic response to the sunset, utterly lacking in imagination. Neither the sentimental effusions of the passenger, nor the solemn dullness of the pilot could satisfactorily express Twain's way of looking at the world. He needed a style that would be imaginative yet realistic and untrammelled by conventional notions of 'fine writing'. He found this style and outlook in his imaginative rediscovery of childhood, in the child's vision of life. As a contrast to the sunset on the river passage, here is Twain describing a different river scene; the arrival of a steamboat in the Hannibal of his boyhood.

21

Once a day a cheap, gaudy packet arrived upward from St. Louis, and another downward from Keokuk. Before these events, the day was glorious with expectancy; after them, the day was a dead and empty thing. Not only the boys, but the whole village, felt this. After all these years I can picture that old time to myself now, just as it was then: the white town drowsing in the sunshine of a summer's morning; the streets empty, or pretty nearly so; one or two clerks sitting in front of the Water Street stores, with their splint-bottomed chairs tilted back against

the wall, chins on breasts, hats slouched over their faces, asleep—with shingle shavings enough around to show what broke them down; a sow and a litter of pigs loafing along the sidewalk, doing a good business in watermelon rinds and seeds; two or three lonely little freight piles scattered about the 'levee'; a pile of 'skids' on the slope of the stone-paved wharf, and the fragrant town drunkard asleep in the shadow of them; two or three wood flats at the head of the wharf, but nobody to listen to the peaceful lapping of the wavelets against them; the great Mississippi, the majestic, the magnificent Mississippi, rolling its mile-wide tide along, shining in the sun; the dense forest away on the other side; the 'point' above the town, and the 'point' below, bounding the river-glimpse and turning it into a sort of sea, and withal a very still and brilliant and lone one. Presently a film of dark smoke appears above one of those remote 'points'; instantly a Negro drayman, famous for his quick eye and prodigious voice, lifts up the cry, 'S-t-e-a-m-boat a-comin'!' and the scene changes! The town drunkard stirs, the clerks wake up, a furious clatter of drays follows, every house and store pours out a human contribution, and all in a twinkling the dead town is alive and moving. Drays, carts, men, boys, all go hurrying from many quarters to a common center, the wharf. Assembled there, the people fasten their eyes upon the coming boat as upon a wonder they are seeing for the first time. And the boat is rather a handsome sight, too. She is long and sharp and trim and pretty; she has two tall, fancy-topped chimneys, with a gilded device of some kind swung between them; a fanciful pilothouse, all glass and 'gingerbread,' perched on top of the 'texas' deck behind them; the paddle-boxes are gorgeous with a picture or with gilded rays above the boat's name; the boiler deck, the hurricane deck, and the texas deck are fenced and ornamented with clean white railings; there is a flag gallantly flying from the jackstaff; the furnace doors are open and the
66

fires glaring bravely; the upper decks are black with passengers; the captain stands by the big bell, calm, imposing, the envy of all; great volumes of the blackest smoke are rolling and tumbling out of the chimneys—a husbanded grandeur created with a bit of pitch pine just before arriving at a town; the crew are grouped on the forecastle; the broad stage is run far out over the port bow, and an envied deck hand stands picturesquely on the end of it with a coil of rope in his hand; the pent steam is screaming through the gauge cocks; the captain lifts his hand, a bell rings, the wheels stop; then they turn back, churning the water to foam, and the steamer is at rest. Then such a scramble as there is to get aboard, and to get ashore, and to take in freight and to discharge freight, all at one and the same time; and such a yelling and cursing as the mates facilitate it all with! Ten minutes later the steamer is under way again, with no flag on the jack-staff and no black smoke issuing from the chimneys. After ten more minutes the town is dead again, and the town drunkard asleep by the skids once more.

Life on the Mississippi, ch. 4

Here is the alternative to sentimental posturing and dull utilitarianism; a description imbued with a fondly recollected and felt quality of life. Despite the clarity of the prose, the mood of the passage is romantic, even nostalgic; it recalls the wonder of the 'old time' of childhood, when the 'white town' was flooded in bright summer sunshine. It suggests a time of innocence and happiness, when life was made wonderful through the appearance of a gaudy steam boat. Before the boat is sighted, the village is in a state of tranquil apathy; the clerks with hats 'slouched over their faces' doze on their chairs, the town drunk sleeps on the wharf, while the only sign of life on the street is a sow and her litter 'loafing' among the

67

garbage. It is a lazy, relaxed scene, set against the 'peaceful lapping' of the river, but there is also perhaps a suggestion of melancholy and sadness in the memory which is 'very still and brilliant and lone'—rather like a photograph from a lost childhood. But the village itself is no pastoral idyll; it is full of precisely remembered detail about drunks, clerks in 'splint-bottomed' chairs, freight piles, 'skids', pigs and water-melon rinds—objects that are neither conventionally 'beautiful' nor 'picturesque', but were part of Twain's boyhood experience in Hannibal. The lethargy of the scene is dramatically broken when the Negro drayman's cry announces that the steam boat is in sight. The sleepers awake and the village is now full of confused movement. In the earlier scene of tranquillity the reader had been guided slowly over the town to the river in one long sentence. But now the sentences are shorter and more dramatic; nouns are tumbled on top of each other ('Drays, carts, men, boys'), and the movement is dominated by verbs of action ('lifts', 'stirs', 'pours', 'follows').

The boat itself which occasions all this excitement is not magnificent—it is only a 'cheap, gaudy packet'. Yet Twain captures the sense of wonder it creates in the villagers and himself—they look at it 'as upon a wonder they are seeing for the first time'. In contrast to the white sleepy town the boat is gaudy and colourful, but something of a sham. Twain avoids sentimentality by an ironic distancing of himself from the events he describes. Thus he remembers the boat as being 'trim and pretty', but it is also 'gilded', 'all glass and gingerbread', like something from a fair-ground. Like Tom Sawyer and Hank Morgan, both supreme showmen, the boat and its crew strive after melodramatic effects. The flags are flying, the furnace doors are open, smoke bellows out in 'husbanded grandeur', the captain takes up an attitude of dignified authority by the bell, and even the 'envied deck hand' poses for the benefit of his audience. The arrival of the boat heralds a spectacular show which entertains the dullness of the village for a brief period, before it leaves, and the people once again sink back into apathy. The boat is both genuine and a fraud; genuine to the villagers and the imagination of childhood, but a fraud to the mature vision of Mark Twain who looks on it with amused irony.

The next two extracts illustrate the development of Twain's style between *The Adventures of Tom Sawyer* and *Huckleberry Finn*. Both passages describe a similar episode: a violent summer thunder storm on Jackson's Island.

22

About midnight Joe awoke, and called the boys. There was a brooding oppressiveness in the air that seemed to bode something. The boys huddled themselves together and sought the friendly companionship of the fire, though the dull dead heat of the breathless atmosphere was stifling. They sat still, intent and waiting. The solemn hush continued. Beyond the light of the fire everything was swallowed up in the blackness of darkness. Presently there came a quivering glow that vaguely revealed the foliage for a moment and then vanished. By and by another came, a little stronger. Then another. Then a faint moan came sighing through the branches of the forest and the boys felt a fleeting breath upon their cheeks, and shuddered with the fancy that the Spirit of the Night had gone by. There was a pause. Now a weird flash turned night into day and showed every little grass blade, separate and distinct, that grew about their feet. And it showed three white, startled faces, too. A deep peal of thunder went rolling and tumbling down the heavens and lost itself in sullen rumblings in the distance. A sweep of chilly air passed by, rustling all the leaves and snowing the flaky ashes broadcast about the fire. Another fierce glare lit up the forest and an instant crash followed that seemed to rend the treetops right over the boys' heads. They clung together in terror, in the thick gloom that followed. A few big raindrops fell pattering upon the leaves.

'Quick! boys, go for the tent!' exclaimed Tom.

They sprang away, stumbling over roots and among vines in the dark, no two plunging in the same direction. A furious blast roared through the trees, making everything sing as it went. One blinding flash after another came, and peal on peal of deafening thunder. And now a drenching rain poured down and the rising hurricane drove it in sheets along the ground. The boys cried out to each other, but the roaring wind and the booming thunderblasts drowned their voices utterly. However, one by one they straggled in at last and took shelter under the tent, cold, scared, and streaming with water; but to have company in misery seemed something to be grateful for. They could not talk, the old sail flapped so furiously, even if the other noises would have allowed them. The tempest rose higher and higher, and presently the sail tore loose from its fastenings and went winging away on the blast. The boys seized each others' hands and fled, with many tumblings and bruises, to the shelter of a great oak that stood upon the riverbank. Now the battle was at its highest. Under the ceaseless conflagration of lightning that flamed in the skies, everything below stood out in clean-cut and shadowless distinctness: the bending trees, the billowy river, white with foam, the driving spray of spume flakes, the dim outlines of the high bluffs on the other side, glimpsed through the drifting cloud rack and the slanting veil of rain. Every little while some giant tree yielded the fight and fell crashing through the younger growth; and the unflagging thunderpeals came now in

70

earsplitting explosive bursts, keen and sharp, and unspeakably appalling. The storm culminated in one matchless
effort that seemed likely to tear the island to pieces, burn
it up, drown it to the treetops, blow it away, and deafen
every creature on it, all at one and the same moment.
It was a wild night for homeless young heads to be out in.

The Adventures of Tom Sawyer, ch. 16

23

We spread the blankets inside for a carpet, and eat our
dinner in there. We put all the other things handy at the
back of the cavern. Pretty soon it darkened up, and begun
to thunder and lighten; so the birds was right about it.
Directly it begun to rain, and it rained like all fury, too,
and I never see the wind blow so. It was one of these
regular summer storms. It would get so dark that it looked
all blue-black outside, and lovely; and the rain would
thrash along by so thick that the trees off a little ways
looked dim and spider-webby; and here would come a blast
of wind that would bend the trees down and turn up the
pale underside of the leaves; and then a perfect ripper
of a gust would follow along and set the branches to tossing their arms as if they was just wild; and next, when it
was just about the bluest and blackest—*fst!* it was as
bright as glory, and you'd have a little glimpse of treetops a-plunging about away off yonder in the storm,
hundreds of yards further than you could see before; dark
as sin again in a second, and now you'd hear the thunder
let go with an awful crash, and then go rumbling, grumbling, tumbling, down the sky towards the under side of
the world, like rolling empty barrels down-stairs—where
it's long stairs and they bounce a good deal, you know.

Huckleberry Finn, ch. 9

In the passage from *Tom Sawyer*, written soon after 'Old Times', Twain reverts to conventional attitudes and descriptive techniques. Although the passage describes a group of children terrified by a violent storm, it is told by the voice of a sophisticated adult narrator, who stands well away from the events and adopts a patronizing air. The children lack individual identities, and in the final sentence they are like stereotyped innocent waifs from sentimental Sunday school books. There is no attempt made here to say what the storm felt like from the point of view of the children; the only viewpoint we have is that of the adult commentator, and his style is that of a genteel man of letters. He uses a hackneyed 'poetic' personification, 'Spirit of Night', which would surely never have entered the thoughts of young boys. The events of the storm are described in a vague, inflated and elegantly conventional manner; the stillness before the storm breaks is a 'solemn hush', the sky a 'ceaseless conflagration', the sound of thunder is 'unspeakably appalling', while the boys are surrounded by 'blackness of darkness'. These phrases blur rather than define sharply Twain's meaning, and their elegance calls attention to the language itself, rather than to the thing described. There is here also a lack of relationship between the boys and the storm; Twain is interested in rather obvious melodramatic pictorial spectacles, and the children are almost irrelevant to the scene. Even on the one occasion when Tom does speak (' "Quick! boys, go for the tent!" '), his words sound flat and dead.

When Twain allowed Huck to tell his own story he opened up a new dimension of narrative technique, and Huck's description of the storm is much more vivid than Samuel Clemens's. This is partly due to the fact that Huck is integrated with the landscape; Tom is always an outsider, a small human intruder into the grandeurs of nature whom Twain pities. On the other hand, Huck accepts the storm as a natural phenomenon and instead of fleeing in terror he sits down to eat. This is a far better piece of descriptive writing than the *Tom Sawyer* passage; here the narrator and scene are both vital and alive; the sky 'darkened up', it rains 'like all fury', Huck sees the rain 'thrash along', the trees are 'a-plunging' and the thunder is 'rumbling, grumbling, tumbling'. Huck's senses are all alive; instead of seeing the storm as a series of literary clichés he feels it in terms of sensuous imagery, leading up to the remarkable image of the thunder and the rolling barrels. Instead of the darkness being the vaguely metaphysical 'Spirit of Night' it is to Huck's apprehension a definite colour—'blue-black'. What had been vaguely 'bending trees' in the *Tom Sawyer* extract are now defined clearly and suggestively. What Huck notices about the trees apart from their violent movement—'bending' does not convey this like 'thrash', 'tossing', 'a-plunging' do—is their ghostliness. They are 'dim and spider-webby' and they show the 'pale underside' of their leaves. Is there not a suggestion of terror here? Even when Huck manufactures a simile—'dark as sin'—it is appropriate to his mind, since his own 'sin' preoccupies him in the book.

The last two extracts in this chapter again describe a similar episode, though each extract has its own viewpoint and style. In the controversial final section of *Huckleberry Finn* the drifting raft has reached Arkansas, where the King and the Duke sell Jim back into slavery at Phelps's farm. When Huck learns what the two frauds have done he sets out for the farm.

24

When I got there it was all still and Sunday-like, and hot and sunshiny—the hands was gone to the fields; and there was them kind of faint dronings of bugs and flies in the air that makes it seem so lonesome and like everybody's dead and gone; and if a breeze fans along and quivers the leaves, it makes you feel mournful, because you feel like it's spirits whispering—spirits that's been dead ever so many years—and you always think they're talking about *you*. As a general thing it makes a body wish *he* was dead, too, and done with it all.

Phelps's was one of these little one-horse cotton plantations; and they all look alike. A rail fence round a two-acre yard; a stile, made out of logs sawed off and up-ended, in steps, like barrels of a different length, to climb over the fence with, and for the women to stand on when they are going to jump onto a horse; some sickly grass-patches in the big yard, but mostly it was bare and smooth, like an old hat with the nap rubbed off; big double log house for the white folks—hewed logs, with the chinks stopped up with mud or mortar, and these mudstripes been whitewashed some time or another; round-log kitchen, with a big broad, open but roofed passage joining it to the house; log smoke-house back of the kitchen; three little log nigger-cabins in a row t'other side of the smoke-house; one little hut all by itself away down against the back fence, and some out-buildings down a piece the other side; ash-hopper, and big kettle to bile soap in, by the little hut; bench by the kitchen door, with bucket of water and a gourd; hound asleep there, in the sun; more hounds asleep, round about; about three shade-trees away off in a corner; some currant bushes and goose-berry bushes in one place by the fence; outside of the fence a garden and a water-melon patch; then the cotton fields begins; and after the fields, the woods.

I went around and clumb over the back stile by the ash-hopper, and started for the kitchen. When I got a little ways, I heard the dim hum of a spinning-wheel wailing along up and sinking along down again; and then I knowed for certain I wished I was dead—for that *is* the lonesomest sound in the whole world.

I went right along, not fixing up any particular plan, but just trusting to Providence to put the right words in my mouth when the time come; for I'd noticed that Providence always did put the right words in my mouth, if I left it alone.

When I got half-way, first one hound and then another got up and went for me, and of course I stopped and faced them, and kept still. And such another pow-wow as they made! In a quarter of a minute I was a kind of a hub of a wheel, as you may say—spokes made out of dogs—circle of fifteen of them packed together around me, with their necks and noses stretched up towards me, a barking and howling; and more a coming; you could see them sailing over fences and around corners from everywheres.

Huckleberry Finn, ch. 32

In this episode Huck is more introverted than he normally is, and while he describes the farm in considerable detail, the description is carefully linked to Huck's mood which is of central importance. Huck is depressed here, and his mood of melancholy is similar to his feelings at the end of chapter 1 when he feels premonitions of death all around him. Instead of analysing his feelings (Huck never says exactly what has made him sad), he relates them closely to sense impressions. Thus the 'faint dronings' of the insects or the quivering of the leaves, even the absence of sound, 'it was all still and Sunday-like', move him not only to melancholia, but to an unsophisticated form of death-wish. The 'dim hum' of the spinning wheel, he relates to loneliness, and he confesses, 'I wished I was dead'. Although perhaps Clemens would not have acknowledged this, Huck is responding here to a basic transcendentalist notion about nature. Emerson summed up the belief when he declared in his essay on 'Nature': 'Nature is the symbol of spirit'. Huck describes the farm in matter-of-fact detail. The impression he gives of the place is not very attractive; it seems crude, dull and dingy—it has 'sickly' grass patches, the mud filling had been whitewashed 'some time or another', and he likens the place to an old worn hat. But apart from the dullness and sadness of the farm, is there not also a suggestion of menace in the last paragraph when Huck is surrounded on all sides by the dogs? The mood of this passage prepares us for what is to follow in the novel, and perhaps Huck's mood of sadness stems from this barely recognized knowledge that the quest for freedom is at an end, and even if he can free Jim from the bondage they have no chance of ultimate escape; he has returned to the dull and mean values of 'civilization'.

Though the happenings at Phelps's farm are imaginary, the farm itself was based on Clemens's memories of childhood visits to his uncle, John Quarles. The farm remained in his imagination all his life, and when, near the end of his life, he composed his *Autobiography*, he remembered with an old man's nostalgia the Quarles farm which seemed to him a lost Eden of innocence and happiness.

25

The life which I led there with my cousins was full of charm, and so is the memory of it yet. I can call back the solemn twilight and mystery of the deep woods, the

earthy smells, the faint odors of the wild flowers, the
sheen of rain-washed foliage, the rattling clatter of drops
when the wind shook the trees, the far-off hammering of
woodpeckers and the muffled drumming of wood pheasants
in the remoteness of the forest, the snapshot glimpses of
disturbed wild creatures scurrying through the grass—I
can call it all back and make it as real as it ever was, and
as blessed. I can call back the prairie, and its loneliness
and peace, and a vast hawk hanging motionless in the
sky, with his wings spread wide and the blue of the vault
showing through the fringe of their end feathers. I can
see the woods in their autumn dress, the oaks purple, the
hickories washed with gold, the maples and the sumachs
luminous with crimson fires, and I can hear the rustle
made by the fallen leaves as we plowed through them. I
can see the blue clusters of wild grapes hanging among
the foliage of the saplings, and I remember the taste of
them and the smell. I know how the wild blackberries
looked, and how they tasted, and the same with the paw-
paws, the hazelnuts, and the persimmons; and I can feel
the thumping rain, upon my head, of hickory nuts and
walnuts when we were out in the frosty dawn to scramble
for them with the pigs, and the gusts of wind loosed them
and sent them down. I know the stain of blackberries,
and how pretty it is, and I know the stain of walnut hulls,
and how little it minds soap and water, also what grudged
experience it had of either of them. I know the taste of
maple sap, and when to gather it, and how to arrange the
troughs and the delivery tubs, and how to boil down the
juice, and how to hook the sugar after it is made, also how
much better hooked sugar tastes than any that is honestly
come by, let bigots say what they will. I know how a
prize watermelon looks when it is sunning its fat
rotundity among pumpkin vines and 'simblins'; I know
how to tell when it is ripe without 'plugging' it; I know
how inviting it looks when it is cooling itself in a tub of
water under the bed, waiting; I know how it looks when

77

it lies on the table in the sheltered great floor space between house and kitchen, and the children gathered for the sacrifice and their mouths watering; I know the crackling sound it makes when the carving knife enters its end, and I can see the split fly along in front of the blade as the knife cleaves its way to the other end; I can see its halves fall apart and display the rich red meat and the black seeds, and the heart standing up, a luxury fit for the elect; I know how a boy looks behind a yard-long slice of that melon, and I know how he feels; for I have been there.

The Autobiography of Mark Twain,
ed. Charles Neider, ch. 4

This passage is an attempt to call back what Twain spoke of elsewhere in his *Autobiography* as 'the pathetic past, the beautiful past, the dear and lamented past', but the attempt is only partially successful. Is there a note of desperation in the insistent 'I can'? The recalled images flow along rather like the stream of consciousness—the sentences are long and the scenes pile up one on top of the other held together only by Twain's memory. As with Huck Finn, emotions and feelings are presented in terms of sensory experience; yet there is something missing here, the ability to translate experience into language. Behind the rhetorical assurance lies a doubt, and, although Twain tells us he knows how various things looked and tasted and smelled, we have in the end only his rhetoric to believe in.

Irony and satire

Huckleberry Finn is the turning point in Clemens's career. It constitutes his greatest achievement as a humorous writer, yet it is also a deeply pessimistic book that prepares for the bitterness and disillusion that characterize his later work. The journey of Huck and Jim on their fragile raft reveals their developing love and responsibility for each other, along with a liberation of their senses and emotions from the slavery of conventional morality. But the hope of freedom that sustains their journey down the river vanishes as Cairo is lost in the fog, and by the time he reaches Phelps's farm Huck realizes that their freedom has been betrayed: 'After all this long journey,... here it was all come to nothing, everything all busted up and ruined,...' (ch. 31). In the last section of the novel Huck wearily submits to the tedious farce devised by Tom Sawyer, in which Jim's humanity is mocked and humiliated, then he is offered a false and unrealistic freedom by the 'authorities'. The novel ends where it began, amid the cruel inanities of 'civilization', where truth has surrendered to plausibility, and where a sickly veneer of sentimentality covers over grossness, violence and deceit. Shortly after he had completed *Huckleberry Finn*, Clemens wrote to Howells expressing in graphic terms his contempt for the human race in general: 'Isn't human nature the most consummate sham and lie that ever was invented? Isn't man a creature to be ashamed of in pretty much all his aspects? Is he really fit for anything but to be stood up on a street corner as a convenience for dogs?' The feeling expressed in this letter —that the human race is disgusting and obscene—has its imaginative origins in the scenes of violence and cruelty that permeate *Huckleberry Finn*. In the next extract Huck witnesses a cold-blooded killing in the main street of Bricksville, when Boggs, a loud-mouthed but harmless drunk, is shot down by the town's leading 'gentleman', Colonel Sherburn.

26

He cussed away with all his might, and throwed his hat down in the mud and rode over it, and pretty soon away he went a-raging down the street again, with his gray hair a-flying. Everybody that could get a chance at him tried their best to coax him off of his horse so they could lock him up and get him sober; but it warn't no use— up the street he would tear again, and give Sherburn another cussing. By and by somebody says:

'Go for his daughter!—quick, go for his daughter; sometimes he'll listen to her. If anybody can persuade him, she can.'

So somebody started on a run. I walked down street a ways and stopped. In about five or ten minutes here comes Boggs again, but not on his horse. He was a-reeling across the street towards me, bareheaded, with a friend on both sides of him a-holt of his arms and hurrying him along. He was quiet, and looked uneasy; and he warn't hanging back any, but was doing some of the hurrying himself. Somebody sings out:

'Boggs!'

I looked over there to see who said it, and it was that Colonel Sherburn. He was standing perfectly still in the street, and had a pistol raised in his right hand—not aiming it, but holding it out with the barrel tilted up towards the sky. The same second I see a young girl coming on the run, and two men with her. Boggs and the men turned round to see who called him, and when they see the pistol the men jumped to one side, and the pistol-barrel come down slow and steady to a level— both barrels cocked. Boggs throws up both of his hands and says, 'O Lord, don't shoot!' Bang! goes the first shot, and he staggers back, clawing at the air—bang! goes the second one, and he tumbles backwards onto the ground, heavy and solid, with his arms spread out. That young girl screamed out and comes rushing, and down she throws herself on her father, crying, and saying, 'Oh, he's killed him, he's killed him!' The crowd closed up around them, and shouldered and jammed one another, with their necks stretched, trying to see, and people on the inside trying to shove them back and shouting,

'Back, back! give him air, give him air!'

Colonel Sherburn he tossed his pistol onto the ground, and turned around on his heels and walked off.

They took Boggs to a little drug store, the crowd pressing around just the same, and the whole town following, and I rushed and got a good place at the window, where I was close to him and could see in. They laid him on the floor and put one large Bible under his head, and opened another one and spread it on his breast; but they tore open his shirt first, and I seen where one of the bullets went in. He made about a dozen last gasps, his breast lifting the Bible up when he drawed in his breath, and letting it down again when he breathed it out—and after that he laid still; he was dead. Then they pulled his daughter away from him, screaming and crying, and took her off. She was about sixteen, and very sweet and gentle looking, but awful pale and scared.

Well, pretty soon the whole town was there, squirming and scrouging and pushing and shoving to get at the window and have a look, but people that had the places wouldn't give them up, and folks behind them was saying all the time, 'Say, now, you've looked enough, you fellows; 'taint right and 'taint fair, for you to stay thar all the time, and never give nobody a chance; other folks has their rights as well as you.'

There was considerable jawing back, so I slid out, thinking maybe there was going to be trouble. The streets was full, and everybody was excited. Everybody that seen the shooting was telling how it happened, and there was a big crowd packed around each one of these fellows, stretching their necks and listening. One long lanky man, with long hair and a big white fur stove-pipe hat on the back of his head, and a crooked-handled cane, marked out the places on the ground where Boggs stood, and where Sherburn stood, and the people following him around from one place to t'other and watching everything he done, and bobbing their heads to show they understood, and stooping a little and resting their hands on their thighs to watch him mark the places on the ground with his cane; and then he stood up straight and stiff where Sherburn had stood, frowning and having his hat-brim down over his eyes, and sung out, 'Boggs!' and then fetched his cane down slow to a level, and says 'Bang!' staggered backwards, says 'Bang!' again, and fell down flat on his back. The people that had seen the thing said he done it perfect; said it was just exactly the way it all happened. Then as much as a dozen people got out their bottles and treated him.

Well, by-and-by somebody said Sherburn ought to be lynched. In about a minute everybody was saying it; so away they went, mad and yelling, and snatching down every clothes-line they come to, to do the hanging with.

Huckleberry Finn, ch. 21

The killing is apparently brought about by Boggs's drunken abuse of Colonel Sherburn earlier in the chapter; but the revenge is out of all proportion to the insult, and Boggs is in reality a victim of Sherburn's arrogance and contempt. Boggs is a drunken buffoon, as the description of him raging over his hat implies, but he is also a very frightened old man who is shot down when he is 'quiet', 'uneasy' and 'hurrying himself' to escape. Twain also attempts to evoke our sympathy for Boggs by having him appeal for mercy to Sherburn, and by introducing the rather sentimental figure of Boggs's 'sweet and gentle' daughter who sees her father killed. Colonel Sherburn, on the other hand, is depicted here as an inhuman monster. The act of murder is deliberate and cold-blooded; Sherburn speaks only one word to gain Boggs's attention, carefully takes aim, shoots once, then shoots again to make certain he has killed his victim. Finally he throws his gun on the ground and turns on his heel in a gesture of contempt. He feels no strong emotion and experiences no remorse; it is as if he has killed a rat or some similar vermin. The reaction of the crowd to the murder is as disturbing as Colonel Sherburn's arrogance. Earlier in the chapter Twain had described the loafers of Bricksville engaged in acts of premeditated cruelty: they torture a sow by setting dogs on her; they set fire to stray dogs or run them to death on the street. The death of Boggs is a similar experience for them; they value it as if it were the King's 'funeral orgy', a third rate melodrama performed to relieve their boredom and stupidity. The death of Boggs has a histrionic quality about it, and Sherburn acts as if he were a Villain in a Victorian melodrama, while the crowd treat the murder with prurient curiosity—as if they were witnessing a stage production. They 'closed up' around the dying Boggs with their necks 'stretched'; when they see the wounds they do nothing but gape and hasten his end with a Bible! Even when he is dead they are 'squirming and scrouging and pushing and shoving' to see the body; again the description suggests rats or similar vermin. That the death is seen by the mob as a form of amusement is reinforced by the grotesque spectacle of the man with the 'white fur stovepipe' miming the killing in the street; and although the performance is inept as well as gruesome the mob applaud the performance and reward him with liquor. But the mob is fickle as well as cruel and unfeeling; at the end of the passage they have illogically turned against Sherburn who had provided their melodrama; the 'mad and yelling' audience now prepares to engage in a further melodrama. The human spectacle in the passage is governed by violence, cruelty, arrogance and unreason; it prepares for Huck's rejection of 'civilization' at the end of the novel, and for Twain's later denunciation of what he termed 'the damned human race'.

Huckleberry Finn is steeped in terror and dominated by the fear and tragedy of slavery; yet it is also a comic novel told from the humorous and often lyrically beautiful viewpoint of a boy. If we turn to *Pudd'nhead Wilson* written nearly ten years later, slavery is still the central issue of the fiction, but the humour and lyricism have gone, and we are in the sardonic world of 'Pudd'nhead Wilson's Calendar': 'Whoever has lived long enough to find out what life is, knows how deep a debt of gratitude we owe to Adam, the first great benefactor of our race. He brought death into the world.' (*Pudd'nhead Wilson*, ch. 3.) The comedy in the novel is riddled with irony and grotesque paradoxes, as the following extract illustrates. The scene is the sleepy village of Dawson's Landing, a distorted version of Hannibal, ruled over by slave owning 'gentry', the Driscolls and Essexes. Here Percy Northumberland Driscoll deals with dishonesty among his slaves.

27

The next day—that is to say, on the fourth of September —something occurred which profoundly impressed Roxana. Mr. Driscoll missed another small sum of money —which is a way of saying that this was not a new thing, but had happened before. In truth, it had happened three times before. Driscoll's patience was exhausted. He was a fairly humane man toward slaves and other animals; he was an exceedingly humane man toward the erring of his own race. Theft he could not abide, and plainly there was a thief in his house. Necessarily the thief must be one of his Negroes. Sharp measures must be taken. He called his servants before him. There were three of these, besides Roxy; a man, a woman, and a boy twelve years old. They were not related. Mr. Driscoll said:

'You have all been warned before. It has done no good. This time I will teach you a lesson. I will sell the thief. Which of you is the guilty one?'

They all shuddered at the threat, for here they had a good home, and a new one was likely to be a change for the worse. The denial was general. None had stolen any-thing—not money, anyway—a little sugar, or cake, or honey, or something like that, that 'Marse Percy wouldn't mind or miss,' but not money—never a cent of money. They were eloquent in their protestations, but Mr. Driscoll was not moved by them. He answered each in turn with a stern 'Name the thief!'

The truth was, all were guilty but Roxana; she sus-pected that the others were guilty, but she did not know them to be so. She was horrified to think how near she had come to being guilty herself; she had been saved in the nick of time by a revival in the colored Methodist

Church, a fortnight before, at which time and place she
'got religion.' The very next day after that gracious
experience, while her change of style was fresh upon her
and she was vain of her purified condition, her master
left a couple of dollars lying unprotected on his desk, and
she happened upon that temptation when she was polish-
ing around with a dustrag. She looked at the money awhile
with a steadily rising resentment, then she burst out with:

'Dad blame dat revival, I wisht it had 'a' be'n put off
till tomorrow!'

Then she covered the tempter with a book, and another
member of the kitchen cabinet got it. She made this
sacrifice as a matter of religious etiquette; as a thing
necessary just now, but by no means to be wrested into a
precedent; no, a week or two would limber up her piety,
then she would be rational again, and the next two dollars
that got left out in the cold would find a comforter—
and she could name the comforter.

Was she bad? Was she worse than the general run of
her race? No. They had an unfair show in the battle of
life, and they held it no sin to take military advantage
of the enemy—in a small way; in a small way, but not in
a large one. They would smouch provisions from the
pantry whenever they got a chance; or a brass thimble,
or a cake of wax, or an emery bag, or a paper of needles,
or a silver spoon, or a dollar bill, or small articles of
clothing, or any other property of light value; and so far
were they from considering such reprisals sinful, that
they would go to church and shout and pray the loudest
and sincerest with their plunder in their pockets. A farm
smokehouse had to be kept heavily padlocked, for even
the colored deacon himself could not resist a ham when
Providence showed him in a dream, or otherwise, where
such a thing hung lonesome, and longed for someone to
love. But with a hundred hanging before him, the deacon
would not take two—that is, on the same night. On
frosty nights the humane Negro prowler would warm the
86

end of a plank and put it up under the cold claws of chickens roosting in a tree; a drowsy hen would step on to the comfortable board, softly clucking her gratitude, and the prowler would dump her into his bag, and later into his stomach, perfectly sure that in taking this trifle from the man who daily robbed him of an inestimable treasure—his liberty—he was not committing any sin that God would remember against him in the Last Great Day.

'Name the thief!'

For the fourth time Mr. Driscoll had said it, and always in the same hard tone. And now he added these words of awful import:

'I give you one minute.' He took out his watch. 'If at the end of that time, you have not confessed, I will not only sell all four of you, but—I will sell you DOWN THE RIVER!'

It was equivalent to condemning them to hell! No Missouri Negro doubted this. Roxy reeled in her tracks, and the color vanished out of her face; the others dropped to their knees as if they had been shot; tears gushed from their eyes, their supplicating hands went up, and three answers came in the one instant.

'I done it!'

'I done it!'

'I done it!—have mercy, marster—Lord have mercy on us po' niggers!'

'Very good,' said the master, putting up his watch, 'I will sell you *here* though you don't deserve it. You ought to be sold down the river.'

The culprits flung themselves prone, in an ecstasy of gratitude, and kissed his feet, declaring that they would never forget his goodness and never cease to pray for him as long as they lived. They were sincere, for like a god he had stretched forth his mighty hand and closed the gates of hell against them. He knew, himself, that he had done a noble and gracious thing, and was privately

87

well pleased with his magnanimity; and that night he set the incident down in his diary, so that his son might read it in after years, and be thereby moved to deeds of gentleness and humanity himself.

Pudd'nhead Wilson, ch. 2

The passage describes slavery in operation; it reveals how the system distorted human values, and debased both the owner and the owned. Percy Driscoll is not a naturally cruel or brutal person; on the contrary, he is described as a 'humane man', which makes his behaviour all the more terrible, since it cannot be seen as an aberration of human nature. His attitude towards slaves—he equates them with animals—is conditioned by his environment and training, and Pudd'nhead Wilson, the sardonic commentator on this fallen world reminds us, 'Training is everything' (ch. 5). The values of Percy Driscoll are bound up with property, money and power, which distort his humanity. We are told, 'Theft he could not abide', but ironically is he not the great thief of the extract, who robs his fellow men of their freedom and humanity? The negro slaves are conditioned to stealing, but the important question is why should they steal trivia like needles, spoons and hens? The answer lies in Twain's statement: 'They had an unfair show in the battle of life.' To steal is an act of independence, a gesture of defiance, a sign that they have not given up the 'battle', but still have the will to live as human beings, instead of being provided for like cattle. Religion is seen as a negative force: when Roxy has 'got religion' she denies her natural impulses and becomes frustrated and guilt-ridden. But the ironic 'purified condition' is only temporary when her instinct for freedom reasserts itself she becomes 'rational' again.

Twain shows remarkable insight into the psychology of

oppressed people, and the passage builds up to a bitterly ironic climax which dramatizes the psychic relationship between the oppressor and the oppressed. When Driscoll threatens the slaves with being sold down the river they are stricken with terror, (the deep South was the nightmare held up before Northern slaves as a punishment for disobedience, laziness etc.) They all confess, debase themselves at Driscoll's feet and beg for mercy. They take part in a bitter drama of servitude; in an 'ecstasy of gratitude' they kiss Driscoll's feet, while he 'like a god' grants them a small mercy. But a god is not human, and by exercising absolute power Driscoll has lost hold of reality. By the end of the passage his distorted mind has persuaded itself that his vile behaviour has been 'gentleness and humanity'.

Pudd'nhead Wilson is an investigation into the nature of slavery, what slavery does to the human psyche, and how slavery is a metaphor for the human condition. The laughter it evokes is bitter and corrosive; the humour is that defined by Satan in *The Mysterious Stranger:*

28

'There spoke the race!' he said; 'always ready to claim what it hasn't got, and mistake its ounce of brass filings for a ton of gold dust. You have a mongrel perception of humor, nothing more; a multitude of you possess that. This multitude see the comic side of a thousand low-grade and trivial things—broad incongruities, mainly; grotesqueries, absurdities, evokers of the horselaugh. The ten thousand high-grade comicalities which exist in the world are sealed from their dull vision. Will a day come when the race will detect the funniness of these juvenilities and laugh at them—and by laughing at them destroy them? For your race, in its poverty, has unquestionably one really effective weapon—laughter. Power, money, persuasion, supplication, persecution—these can lift at a colossal humbug—push it a little—weaken it a little, century by century; but only laughter can blow it to rags and atoms at a blast. Against the assault of laughter nothing can stand. You are always fussing and fighting with your other weapons. Do you ever use that one? No; you leave it lying rusting. As a race, do you ever use it at all? No; you lack sense and the courage.'

The Mysterious Stranger, ch. 10

Although Satan here associates laughter with a sense of humour, what he defines is not humour at all but satire. The laughter of Satan does not mock like the laughter of Mark Twain in *The Innocents Abroad* and *Roughing It*, it destroys and hates like the laughter of *Pudd'nhead Wilson* and Hank Morgan in *A Connecticut Yankee*. Laughter here is a 'weapon' which 'assaults' the 'colossal humbug' of existence, and by so doing 'can blow it to rags and atoms at a blast'. The violence and destructive power of Satan's laughter has little affinity with the self-mockery of Mark Twain; it belongs rather to the violent hopeless world of Hank Morgan the Yankee mechanic who comes as a 'mysterious stranger' to enlighten the darkness of Arthurian England, benighted in chivalry and slavery and superstition. In the next extract Hank Morgan is travelling around England incognito accompanied by his faithful girl companion, Sandy. Everywhere he discovers violence, cruelty, and death, and he realizes that the inhabitants of Arthurian England are living a distorted, barely human existence. Hank finds himself obliged to go to the rescue of a group of noble ladies who Sandy insists are imprisoned in an ogre's castle. The castle he discovers to be a pigsty and the ladies turn out to be forty-five fat sows; but he subscribes to Sandy's delusion, buys the

pigs from their 'ogre' owners, and delivers them from
their enchanted captivity with the following ironic comment: '... when I know that an ostensible hog is a lady,
that is enough for me, I know how to treat her.' (ch. 20).

29

I sent the three men away, and then opened the sty
gate and beckoned Sandy to come—which she did; and
not leisurely, but with the rush of a prairie fire. And when
I saw her fling herself upon those hogs, with tears of
joy running down her cheeks, and strain them to her
heart, and kiss them, and caress them, and call them
reverently by grand princely names, I was ashamed of
her, ashamed of the human race.

We had to drive those hogs home—ten miles; and no
ladies were ever more fickle-minded or contrary. They
would stay on no road, no path; they broke out through
the brush on all sides, and flowed away in all directions,
over rocks, and hills, and the roughest places they could
find. And they must not be struck, or roughly accosted;
Sandy could not bear to see them treated in ways unbecom-
ing their rank. The troublesomest old sow of the lot had to
be called my Lady, and your Highness, like the rest. It is
annoying and difficult to scour around after hogs, in
armor. There was one small countess, with an iron ring
in her snout and hardly any hair on her back, that was the
devil for perversity. She gave me a race of an hour over
all sorts of country, and then we were right where we
had started from, having made not a rod of real progress.
I seized her at last by the tail, and brought her along,
squealing. When I overtook Sandy, she was horrified, and
said it was in the last degree indelicate to drag a countess
by her train.

We got the hogs home just at dark—most of them.
The princess Nerovens de Morganore was missing, and

two of her ladies in waiting: namely, Miss Angela Bohun, and the Demoiselle Elaine Courtemains, the former of these two being a young black sow with a white star in her forehead, and the latter a brown one with thin legs and a slight limp in the forward shank on the starboard side—a couple of the tryingest blisters to drive, that I ever saw. Also among the missing were several mere baronesses—and I wanted them to stay missing; but no, all that *sausage meat* had to be found; so, servants were sent out with torches to scour the woods and hills to that end.

Of course the whole drove was housed in the house, and great guns—well, I never saw anything like it! Nor ever heard anything like it. And never smelt anything like it. It was like an insurrection in a gasometer.

A Connecticut Yankee, ch. 20

The humour in this passage derives from two conflicting ways of looking at the 'ladies' of the enchanted castle. From Hank's commonsense viewpoint the pigs are merely pigs, but for Sandy they are, despite all appearances, the representatives of the aristocracy she has been brought up to revere and adore. The comparison of princesses to sows allows Twain to express his dislike of aristocracy, but the vehemence of his satiric attack is mitigated by the comic extravagance of the scene in which Hank scours over the country addressing the pigs as 'my Lady and your Highness'. The technique Twain employs is one of deflation and reduction in which the hated image is distorted and debased. This description is also, perhaps, an attack on the sentimental ideal of womanhood so prevalent in the nineteenth century and to which Clemens himself subscribed on occasions, notably in the sickly idealism of *Personal Recollections of Joan of Arc*. Sandy is a believer in the ideal of womanhood; Hank sees her kiss and caress the pigs and his reaction is one of shame for her as a representative of the human race. The absurd idealism of Sandy is balanced against the Yankee's brutal lack of sentiment. He sees the pigs as 'sausage meat', and describes 'one small countess, with an iron ring in her snout, and hardly any hair on her back'. There is a Swiftean quality to Twain's humour here : apart from the reference to the stink the aristocracy make, the pigs retain human characteristics—Demoiselle Elaine Courtemains has 'thin legs and a slight limp in the forward shank on the starboard, . . .'. Sandy and Hank are really seeing the same thing when they encounter the pig-ladies, only their viewpoints and attitudes differ.

The contempt that Hank feels for the pig-ladies and for Sandy's adoration of them eventually embraces the whole of Arthur's kingdom. He had come into the primitive pre-industrial world bringing with him the techniques of nineteenth century technology; he had sought to establish industry and communications; he had set up 'Man-factories', and attempted to destroy the ancient powers of chivalry and the established church; he had ridiculed the 'magic' powers of Merlin and established himself as 'The Boss' of the nation. But Hank finds it increasingly difficult to sustain his faith in the democracy he has established. The 'human muck' as he calls the people are not changed despite all the Yankee's innovations; hypocrisy, cruelty and superstition remain ineradicable elements in human nature, and by the end of the book Hank realizes the futility of his quest. His contempt gives way to anger and bitterness, and the novel ends in a holocaust.

30

The sun rose presently and sent its unobstructed splendors

over the land, and we saw a prodigious host moving slowly toward us, with the steady drift and aligned front of a wave of the sea. Nearer and nearer it came, and more and more sublimely imposing became its aspect; yes, all England were there, apparently. Soon we could see the innumerable banners fluttering, and then the sun struck the sea of armor and set it all a-flash. Yes, it was a fine sight; I hadn't ever seen anything to beat it.

At last we could make out details. All the front ranks, no telling how many acres deep, were horsemen— plumed knights in armor. Suddenly we heard the blare of trumpets; the slow walk burst into a gallop, and then —well, it was wonderful to see! Down swept that vast horseshoe wave—it approached the sand belt—my breath stood still; nearer, nearer—the strip of green turf beyond the yellow belt grew narrower—narrower still—became a mere ribbon in front of the horses—then disappeared under their hoofs. Great Scott! Why, the whole front of that host shot into the sky with a thundercrash, and became a whirling tempest of rags and fragments; and along the ground lay a thick wall of smoke that hid what was left of the multitude from our sight.

Time for the second step in the plan of campaign! I touched a button, and shook the bones of England loose from her spine!

In that explosion all our noble civilization-factories went up in the air and disappeared from the earth. It was a pity, but it was necessary. We could not afford to let the enemy turn our own weapons against us.

Now ensued one of the dullest quarter hours I had ever endured. We waited in a silent solitude enclosed by our circles of wire, and by a circle of heavy smoke out-side of these. We couldn't see over the wall of smoke, and we couldn't see through it. But at last it began to shred away lazily, and by the end of another quarter hour the land was clear and our curiosity was enabled to satisfy itself. No living creature was in sight! We now perceived that additions had been made to our defenses. The dynamite had dug a ditch more than a hundred feet wide, all around us, and cast up an embankment some twenty-five feet high on both borders of it. As to destruction of life, it was amazing. Moreover, it was beyond estimate. Of course we could not count the dead, because they did not exist as individuals, but merely as homogeneous protoplasm, with alloys of iron and buttons.

No life was in sight, but necessarily there must have been some wounded in the rear ranks, who were carried off the field under cover of the wall of smoke; there would be sickness among the others—there always is, after an episode like that. But there would be no reinforcements; this was the last stand of the chivalry of England; it was all that was left of the order, after the recent annihilating wars. So I felt quite safe in believing that the utmost force that could for the future be brought against us would be but small; that is, of knights. I therefore issued a congratulatory proclamation to my army in these words:

SOLDIERS, CHAMPIONS OF HUMAN LIBERTY AND EQUALITY: Your General congratulates you! In the pride of his strength and the vanity of his renown, an arrogant enemy came against you. You were ready. The conflict was brief; on your side, glorious. This mighty victory having been achieved utterly without loss, stands without example in history. So long as the planets shall continue to move in their orbits, the BATTLE OF THE SAND BELT will not perish out of the memories of men.
THE BOSS.

I read it well, and the applause I got was very gratifying to me. I then wound up with these remarks:

'The war with the English nation, as a nation, is at an end. The nation has retired from the field and the war. Before it can be persuaded to return, war will have ceased. This campaign is the only one that is going to be

95

fought. It will be brief—the briefest in history. Also the most destructive to life, considered from the standpoint of proportion of casualties to numbers engaged. We are done with the nation; henceforth we deal only with the knights. English knights can be killed, but they cannot be conquered. We know what is before us. While one of these men remains alive, our task is not finished, the war is not ended. We will kill them all.' [Loud and long continued applause.]

A Connecticut Yankee, ch. 43

The world that Hank Morgan came to save in the name of democracy he ends by destroying, and his despair and frustration surely reflect Twain's disillusion with the 'damned human race'. The course of history in this novel is cyclical and repetitive, rather than linear and progressive; it begins with the darkness of an eclipse, and ends amid a wasteland of death brought about by the Yankee's megalomania. The principle of darkness he attempted to eradicate from others he ironically fails to discover within himself. Ultimately Hank's failure, like Clemens's, is a failure of vision and imagination, and this is reflected in his language. Compared with Huck's poetic vernacular, Hank's language is dull indeed; when he describes the chivalry of England he resorts to conventional rhetoric: 'unobstructed splendours', 'sublimely imposing'. Even when he sees the knights blown to pieces, his amazement is expressed in a slang cliché: 'Great Scott!'

There is something unpleasant about Hank's detachment from the scenes of suffering and death he has created; he turns into a God-like figure manipulating and destroying with contempt his puny human adversaries whom he views as 'homogeneous protoplasm'. At the beginning of the extract Hank views the battle as if it were a theatrical entertainment; it is a grandiose spectacle 'wonderful to see', and when the explosion is over he is faced with an interval—'one of the dullest quarter hours I had even endured'. But as the description continues the Yankee reveals not only a lack of pity and sensitivity, but also a growing hubris and megalomania. His speech to his troops is pompous and inflated; it also suggests an insane egotism. This is supported by the final paragraph where the Yankee is obsessed with killing; his threat 'we will kill them all' reveals the terrible destruction of his idealism.

The final extract in this book describes a situation similar to that of Hank Morgan destroying the chivalry of England. Here Satan, the angelic visitor in *The Mysterious Stranger*, creates a mimic world of little men and women for the amusement of Theodor and his young friends. When the little men begin displaying human characteristics Satan destroys them in disgust.

31

Two of the little workmen were quarreling, and in buzzing little bumblebee voices they were cursing and swearing at each other; now came blows and blood; then they locked themselves together in a life-and-death struggle. Satan reached out his hand and crushed the life out of them with his fingers, threw them away, wiped the red from his fingers on his handkerchief, and went on talking where he had left off: 'We cannot do wrong; neither have we any disposition to do it, for we do not know what it is.'

It seemed a strange speech, in the circumstances, but we barely noticed that, we were so shocked and grieved at the wanton murder he had committed—for murder it was, that was its true name, and it was without palliation or excuse, for the men had not wronged him in any

97

way. It made us miserable, for we loved him, and had thought him so noble and so beautiful and gracious, and had honestly believed he was an angel; and to have him do this cruel thing—ah, it lowered him so, and we had had such pride in him. He went right on talking, just as if nothing had happened, telling about his travels, and the interesting things he had seen in the big worlds of our solar system and of other solar systems far away in the remotenesses of space, and about the customs of the immortals that inhabit them, somehow fascinating us, enchanting us, charming us in spite of the pitiful scene that was now under our eyes, for the wives of the little dead men had found the crushed and shapeless bodies and were crying over them, and sobbing and lamenting, and a priest was kneeling there with his hands crossed upon his breast, praying; and crowds and crowds of pitying friends were massed about them, reverently uncovered with their bare heads bowed, and many with the tears running down—a scene which Satan paid no attention to until the small noise of the weeping and praying began to annoy him, then he reached out and took the heavy board seat out of our swing and brought it down and mashed all those people into the earth just as if they had been flies, and went on talking just the same.

An angel, and kill a priest! An angel who did not know how to do wrong, and yet destroys in cold blood hundreds of helpless poor men and women who had never done him any harm! It made us sick to see that awful deed, and to think that none of those poor creatures was prepared except the priest, for none of them had ever heard a mass or seen a church. And we were witnesses; we had seen these murders done and it was our duty to tell, and let the law take its course.

The Mysterious Stranger, ch. 2

Satan is the angelic visitor who appears to the group of boys in medieval Eseldorf to reveal to them the terrible and futile nature of human existence. He is a supernatural spectator for whom human life is an absurd joke; he crushes his mimic men with no compassion or guilt, for he does not possess the curse of human life—the Moral Sense. The tension in this passage lies between the dogmatic amorality of Satan who says, ' "We can do no wrong; ..." ' and the moral scruples of the children when they witness the destruction of the mimic men. The transcendent stranger reveals to the children the terrible absurdity of human existence where nothing exists apart from a dream, and he voices the disillusion that had been evident in Twain's work since the dark insights of *Huckleberry Finn*. Satan's act of destruction of his little adult world is the symbolic act of a writer, who had lost faith in the value of existence; all he can offer is the pity of an uncorrupted child.

Bibliography

Mark Twain's Writings

All Mark Twain's important works are cited below. For a more complete bibliography the reader should consult: (1) *Bibliography of American Literature*, Compiled by Jacob Blanck, vol. 2, Yale University Press, New Haven, 1957. (2) *Literary History of the United States, Bibliography and Supplement*, ed. Thomas H. Johnson, et. al., Macmillan, New York, 1962.

The Celebrated Jumping Frog of Calaveras County, and Other Sketches, (1867).

The Innocents Abroad, (1869). Also: With an Afterword by Leslie Fiedler, (Signet Classics), New American Library, New York, 1966.

Roughing It, (1872). Also: (1) ed. R. W. Paul, Holt, Rinehart & Winston, New York, 1953. (2) With a Foreword by Leonard Kriegel, (Signet Classics), New American Library, New York, 1962.

The Gilded Age, (with Charles Dudley Warner), (1873). Also: (First Novel Library), Cassell, London, 1967. Mark Twain's part of the novel has been published separately: *The Adventures of Colonel Sellers*, ed. Charles Neider, Chatto & Windus, London, 1966.

Sketches New and Old, (1875).

The Adventures of Tom Sawyer, (1876). Also: (1) With an Introduction by L. Trilling, Collier – Macmillan, New York, 1962. (2) With an Afterword by George P. Elliott, (Signet Classics), New American Library, New York, 1959. (3) (The Zodiac Press), Chatto & Windus, London, 1962.

A Tramp Abroad, (1880).

The Prince and the Pauper, (1882). Also: With an Afterword by K. S. Lynn, (Signet Classics), New American Library, New York, 1964.

The Stolen White Elephant and Other Stories, (1882).

Life on the Mississippi, (1883). Also: (1) With an Introduction by Beaver, (The World's Classics), O.U.P., London & New York, 1962. (2) With an Afterword by Leonard Kriegel, (Signet Classics), New American Library, New York, 1961.

The Adventures of Huckleberry Finn, (1884). Also: (1) With an Introduction by Lionel Trilling, Holt Rinehart & Winston, New York, 1948. (2) ed. Henry Nash Smith, (Riverside Edition), Houghton Mifflin, Boston, 1958. (3) ed. Kenneth S. Lynn, Harcourt, Brace & World, New York, 1961. (4) (The Zodiac Press), Chatto & Windus, London, 1963. (5) ed. Peter Coveney, (Penguin English Library), Harmondsworth, 1966. (6) With an Introduction by Leo Marx, Bobbs-Merrill, New York, 1967.

A Connecticut Yankee in King Arthur's Court, (1889). Also: (1) With an Afterword by Edmund Reiss, (Signet Classics), New American Library, New York, 1963. (2) (The Zodiac Press), Chatto & Windus, 1957.

The American Claimant, (1892).

The £1,000,000 Bank Note and Other New Stories, (1893).

The Tragedy of Pudd'nhead Wilson, (1894). Also: (1) With an Introduction by F. R. Leavis, Grove Press, New York, 1955. (2) (Zodiac Press), Chatto & Windus, London, 1955. (3) With a Foreword by Wright Morris, (Signet Classics), New American Library, New York, 1964.

Personal Recollections of Joan of Arc, (1896).

Tom Sawyer Abroad, Tom Sawyer, Detective, and Other Stories, (1896). Also: Collier-Macmillan, New York, 1962.

Following the Equator, (1897). An altered text of this book was published in England under the title *More Tramps Abroad*, (1897).

The Man That Corrupted Hadleyburg and Other Stories and Essays, (1900).

King Leopold's Soliloquy, (1905). Also: (Seven Seas Books), Seven Seas Publishers, Berlin, 1961.

The $30,000 Bequest and Other Stories, (1906).

What is Man? (1906).

Extract from Captain Stormfield's Visit to Heaven, (1909). A more complete version of this book is *Report from Paradise*, ed. Dixon Wecter, Harper, New York, 1952.

The Mysterious Stranger, (1916). Also: With a Foreword by Edmund Reiss, (Signet Classics), New American Library, New York, 1962.

Letters from the Earth, ed. Bernard De Voto, Harper & Row,

New York, 1962. Contains unpublished material from the Mark Twain papers.

Which Was the Dream? and Other Symbolic Writings of the Later Years, ed. John S. Tuckey, University of California Press, Berkeley & Los Angeles, 1967. Previously unpublished material.

AUTOBIOGRAPHY

Mark Twain's Autobiography, ed. A. B. Paine, 2 vols., Harper, New York, 1924. Only about half the manuscript was published by Paine who took on the role of censor.

Mark Twain in Eruption, ed. Bernard De Voto, Harper, New York, 1940. Includes polemical material omitted by Paine.

The Autobiography of Mark Twain, ed. Charles Neider, Harper, New York, 1959; Washington Square Press, New York, 1961; Chatto & Windus, London, 1960. This is the most satisfactory version of the autobiographical writings for the general reader. Neider arranges the material in chronological order.

COLLECTED WORKS

A new collected edition of Mark Twain's writings has been announced by the University of California; the first volumes are due to appear in 1971. In the meanwhile the most definitive collections are: *The Writings of Mark Twain*, (Author's National Edition), 25 vols., New York, 1907-18; *The Writings of Mark Twain*, ed. A. B. Paine, 37 vols., New York, 1922-25.

Other useful collections include: *Mark Twain's Speeches*, Harper, New York, 1923; *Mark Twain's Notebooks*, ed. A. B. Paine, Harper, New York, 1935.

The Complete Short Stories of Mark Twain, ed. Charles Neider, Bantam Classics, New York, 1958.

The Complete Humorous Sketches and Tales of Mark Twain, ed. Charles Neider, Hanover House, Garden City, N.Y., 1961.

The Complete Essays of Mark Twain, ed. Charles Neider, Doubleday, New York, 1963.

LETTERS

There is no complete edition of Mark Twain's letters. Only the most important collections are cited here.

Mark Twain's Letters, ed. A. B. Paine, 2 vols., Harper, New York, 1917; 1 vol., Chatto & Windus, London, 1920.

Mark Twain—Howells Letters, eds. H. N. Smith and W. H. Gibson, 2 vols., University of Harvard, Belknap Press, Cambridge, Mass., 1960.

BIOGRAPHY

ANDREWS, KENNETH R., *Nook Farm: Mark Twain's Hartford Circle*, Harvard University Press, Cambridge, Mass., 1950; Anchor Books, Hamden, Conn., 1967. A detailed account of Mark Twain's social and intellectual environment.

FERGUSON, DE LANCEY, *Mark Twain: Man and Legend*, Indianapolis, Bobbs-Merrill, 1943. A thorough, well-balanced account of Twain's life.

HOWELLS, WILLIAM DEAN, *My Mark Twain*, Harper, New York, 1910. An enthusiastic and judicious appreciation of the man and writer by Twain's closest literary friend.

KAPLAN, JUSTIN, *Mr. Clemens and Mark Twain: A Biography*, Simon & Schuster, New York, 1966. The most complete account of Clemens's life from 1866; well written and thoroughly entertaining.

MELTZER, MILTON, *Mark Twain Himself*, Bonanza Books, New York, 1960. A fascinating pictorial record of Twain's life.

PAINE, A. B., *Mark Twain, A Biography*, 3 vols., Harper, New York, 1912. The authorized biography—uncritical and not completely reliable, but contains material unavailable elsewhere.

WECTER, DIXON, *Sam Clemens of Hannibal*, Houghton Mifflin, Boston, 1952. A study of Twain's childhood and adolescence.

CRITICISM

The following listing is highly selective. For a thorough guide to Mark Twain scholarship the reader should consult: (1) Long, E. H., *Mark Twain Handbook*, Hendricks House, New York, 1957. (2) *Literary History of the United States, Bibliography and Supplement*, Ed. Thomas H. Johnson, et. al., Macmillan, New York, 1962. (3) *Modern Fiction Studies*, 'Mark Twain Special Number', Vol. XIV. No. 1, (Spring, 1968).

BALDANZA, FRANK, *Mark Twain*, (American Authors and Critics), Barnes & Noble, New York, 1961. An intelligent general introduction; contains a useful bibliography.

BLAIR, WALTER, *Native American Humour 1800-1900*, American Book Co., New York, 1937. An anthology illustrating the development of American humour in the nineteenth century. Contains a long scholarly introduction and excellent bibliography. The best work of its kind available.

BLAIR, WALTER, *Mark Twain & Huck Finn*, University of California, Berkeley, 1960. A fascinating, scholarly account of the sources and composition of *Huckleberry Finn*.

BROOKS, VAN WYCK, *The Ordeal of Mark Twain*, Dutton, New York, 1920; Meridian Books, New York, 1955. Argues that Twain's genius was thwarted by American conditions.

COX, JAMES M., *Mark Twain: The Fate of Humour*, Princeton University, Princeton, N.J., 1966. A closely argued and often extremely perceptive study of Twain as a humorist; especially convincing on works prior to *Huckleberry Finn*.

DE VOTO, BERNARD, *Mark Twain's America*, Little, Brown, Boston, 1932. A reply to Van Wyck Brooks: De Voto argues convincingly that Twain was inspired by his American environment.

DE VOTO, BERNARD, *Mark Twain at Work*, Harvard University Press, Cambridge, Mass., 1942. A detailed study of Twain's writing methods.

FONER, PHILIP, *Mark Twain: Social Critic*, International Publishers, New York, 1958. A one sided account of Twain as a radical critic of America.

GRANT, DOUGLAS, *Twain*, (Writers & Critics), Oliver and Boyd, 1962; Grove Press, New York, 1963. A well written general introduction.

LYNN, KENNETH, S., *Mark Twain and Southwestern Humour*, Little, Brown, Boston, 1959. A perceptive study of Twain seen in relationship to an American Comic tradition.

MARKS, BARRY A., *Mark Twain's Huckleberry Finn*, Heath & Co., Boston, 1959. Selected essays which approach the novel from a variety of viewpoints.

ROGERS, FRANKLIN R., *Mark Twain's Burlesque Patterns: As Seen in the Novels and Narratives, 1855-85*, Southern Methodist U.P., Dallas, 1960. A careful study of Twain's use of burlesque.

SMITH, HENRY NASH, *Mark Twain: The Development of a Writer*, Harvard U.P., Cambridge, Mass., 1962. An important study of technique in Twain's work; scholarly and lucid in its interpretations.

SMITH, HENRY NASH, (ed.), *Mark Twain: A Collection of Critical Essays*, (Twentieth Century Views), Prentice-Hall, Englewood Cliffs, N.J., 1963. A useful collection of important Twain criticism.